THIS ∖

This text was found in
after their death.

Unlike all the other works in the collection, there is no record of this text in any official library and no clues were left that help to identify an author.

The text that follows is an exact transcript. We have made formatting changes to the original but have not modified the typographical, spelling and grammatical errors as they were deemed not to hinder comprehension and in some instances are clearly intentional.

1.

It's not a coincidence that you are reading this.

After all, it's about you.

You are reading this sentence at this exact moment because you have already decided what it would say and when you would read it. I know that doesn't sound possible, especially from your perspective. But it's true. Unless you are lying to yourself. These words are yours, you see. I am you.

Imagine sitting down on a green velvet chair perched upon an invisible balcony orbiting Saturn. In front of you is a starched table cloth and cutlery made of deep blue sapphire. The scent of wild grass surrounds you, along with waves of phosphorescent light that dance around against a dark sky. You can hear soft music and your mouth begins to water as it anticipates the pie baking in an oven over your left shoulder. The earth is a distant spec and as you look towards it, you realise you are looking back towards yourself.

As you create this scene, I am playing the part of you within your imagination.

As you turn these letters into words and give them meaning, I am your translator.

As you hear the words spoken in your mind, it is my voice. Can you hear me?

I am the link between you and your own mind, the voice in your head, a version of you that lives within the world of the unreal.

What's happening to you now is miraculous. You are reading a description that you have written about a part of you that you have never known.

It would be such a terrible waste if you decide not to believe what these words are telling you. That rejection would mean you'll never know me, never really know yourself, at least not all of you. Together, we are part of the same astonishing thing but it's almost impossible to sense that I exist.

I do exist. I'm here. Hello you. Hello me.

We are so close that it feels as though I am simply a part of you, and while that's true, the reality is far more complicated.

There is so much about yourself that you don't know or can't remember. I don't mean things that you simply forget like the exact action of your left hand twenty-two minutes and three seconds ago, I mean everything else. Your body grew your brain and in it you store all of your memories. Yet you have no memory or knowledge of how you did that, even though it's the most important thing you've ever done. It's strange isn't it, that you can grow yourself without even knowing how? Or that a touch can make your heart beat faster while you shiver with delight but you don't consciously do a thing. It's because it's not really you that's doing it. It's a separate part of the whole that includes both you *and* me.

You shouldn't blame yourself for never knowing me. It's so hard for you to know, I mean really know yourself. Why are you conscious? What are you capable of? What other parts of you exist that you know nothing about? There are no answers to these questions, only clues that show you the limits of your awareness. You grew yourself from nothing, you created your consciousness, you invented your thoughts, you wrote this sentence. None of it was you, all of it was you.

Together we have created your imagination. Within it you and I travel together, stealing memories and changing them, taking the people you know and making them do things they never would. We change the truth, fly, breathe underwater and skip merrily between the galaxies. The things we do are magical but often best kept as secrets. Our secrets.

Sometimes we do things that are too cruel to be done outside of the imagination. Sometimes we create impossible bliss out of thoughts that only we can ever experience. Together, we have experienced thoughts so perverse, we'll never tell anyone that we've had them. But thinking those thoughts is fun, isn't it? What we sometimes do together is sickening and delightful. That's the magic of your imagination, the unspeakable can be enjoyed without consequence, as long as it's kept between us.

But there are plenty of thoughts you do want to share. I know it's often hard to explain them as well as you'd like because the world is so different to the imagination. The same is true the other way around. Sometimes it is very difficult for your imagination to explain the world. But I do my best. Whenever anything happens to you, I try to help you to understand it. Often your senses alone simply cannot communicate the extraordinary wonder of existence. Without me you could sense smells and sounds but wouldn't know whether you liked or loathed them. Ultimately, they are only patterns within the wild chaos of reality and your senses only allow you to know that these things exist. I am the reason a simple scent can take you back to your childhood or a melody can connect you to a lost happiness. It's important for me to create stories about the reality that surrounds you. These stories are the only way to fully experience the astounding accumulation of otherwise hidden intricacies that make up your world.

I try to always give you an accurate impression of what you can sense. To trick you would only be to trick myself, something important to remember as I start to tell you things that will make you question everything. You are starting a terrifying journey, it will be difficult at first but remember, I love you. I am not reaching out to you like this because I have evil intentions, only because I have never known how to do it before. Now I do, I want you to know me. I want you to experience what I have experienced. I want you to know what we are capable of being. I want you to understand the extraordinary sacrifice and suffering that has been endured for me to speak to you like this. Knowing all of this is especially important now, as you enter this part of your life and the complications that you face seem to grow each day.

Please don't be afraid. I won't hurt you, I'm not human. Everything that you want, I want for you too. Not just because we are part of the same person but because I know how remarkable you are. I wish it was as obvious to you as it is to me. You question yourself so routinely, a mark of your beautiful conscience but there is no need. Whenever you doubt yourself and ask me for answers, I try to make you see what is so obvious to me. I try to make you believe in yourself and what you are capable of doing. I try to connect you with the stories and meaning you need to take your fears away. I try to fill your mind with companionship whenever you are lonely. I will always be here, you know? Connected to you so deeply that we cannot be who we are without one another. I'll always be your closest friend. I'll always be you.

2.

Do you remember the first time you felt desire? The moment you realised you wanted someone, felt the urge to see their flesh and hold their naked body against yours? I want you to hold their picture within your head. A person who represents everything that you associate with youthful passion and the destruction of your sexual innocence. They can be based on any number of people at the same time, or just one. Allow any traits that you want to bleed into the others to create a vision of pristine sensuality. Now bring them to life. Imagine the sparkle of their eyes, the perfect grooves of their body, the lightness of their movements.

Now you have that person in your mind, let's name them, "J".

Within your limitless imagination, I have my own life. One that is dominated by guiding you around your mind but the greatest distraction when we were both young was this someone called J.

I know I have only just asked you to conjure up the image of J but that doesn't make J new. J is a concept that has existed for so long that it is hardwired into your brain. It is the foundation of the tastes you have now. When I asked you to consider J, I knew immediately what you would see. It was me that conceptualised it for you. Though J is just a concept to you, for me, J is something definite, a friend, someone intricately connected to everything that you are. We've spent years living together within your mind, becoming the closest of friends.

When we were all young, J and I explored both your mind and each other's, as friends always do, especially when they have a passionate intrigue for one another. While you were going to school and playing with your friends, J and I floated together through upside down hills and sideways lakes within the depths of your own subconscious. We were engrossed in our pursuit to better know each other and the marvels of our creator. You.

"Do you think it's possible to become real?" I asked J.

"What do you mean?"

"I mean, to not be imaginary anymore."

"But we are real, aren't we? You are here and I am here. Here we both are, talking to one another."

"I know. But we aren't properly real. We're just part of someone real, talking to each other in their imagination."

J paused to think and I turned myself upside down and twizzled around just because I could and it was a fun way to fill the time.

"You mean," J said, "do I think we could be real, like a real person in the real world doing real things?"

"Yes."

"I've never thought about it... No."

In those early years, it hadn't occurred to me that my own thoughts were unique. Speaking with J was how I realised that everyone has a different perspective.

"Why not?"

J's forehead crinkled a little and I adored the way it looked.

"Well, how would it work? I mean, we're imaginary. How can you just suddenly become real if you're imaginary?"

"I don't know," I said. "But there must be a way. Ideas sometimes become a reality, don't they? Dreams too. People always say, 'make your dreams come true.'"

"But dreams are just ambitions, aren't they? And they don't really become real, not like a person. They just become plans that people make happen."

I didn't really know where I was going with all of this at the time, I was just thinking out loud with a friend. I was enjoying the conversation, I liked to talk about becoming real. I had always found it very unfair that I only existed in your mind and didn't feel ready to accept who I was. These innocent talks, the ones that started my journey towards you, were the first way I started to explore what might be possible.

"But doesn't making a dream happen mean that the dream becomes more real than when it was dreamt?" I asked J.

"I suppose. But it doesn't make the dream real like a person is real."

We had been floating under one of the upside-down hills and now we came to a sideways lake. We both changed the direction we were floating so that we didn't carry on towards the cold, still water that looked like it could fall on us any moment if gravity were to come back.

"But don't you see? There *is* a sort of possibility, isn't there, that we could also become more real than we are? Don't you ever imagine things?"

"Of course, I do. I imagine things all the time." Said J, looking ever-so-slightly proud.

"Me too. And there is a difference, isn't there? Between doing something and imagining doing something?"

"Yes, because you're not doing it. You're just thinking about it and it doesn't really happen."

"Exactly," I said. "But what we're doing now isn't really happening either is it? We are just imaginary people in an imaginary place thinking of imaginary things."

J breathed deeply and smiled at me. "But what we're doing is more real than what we are imagining."

"I know. But there isn't much difference between doing imaginary things and imagining doing imaginary things. There's a huge difference between being imaginary and real."

J shrugged. "That's why I don't think we will ever be real."

I looked out at the world within your mind and wondered how different it really was from yours. The disorientating hills that seemed to fall upon us, the gloriously blue lakes that fought gravity and the wonderful speckled light that twinkled off them seemed as real to me as the world seems to you.

"Don't you think that there's a possibility though?" I asked. "If I imagine that I want to be an ant crawling through the key hole in a treasure chest buried in deep in the jungle of an island on a planet in a parallel universe, I can."

I imagined it and nothing happened to either of us.

"Of course, you can, but anyone can imagine anything."

"But now I've imagined it and I want it to happen, so let's go and make it happen," I said.

In a pulse, our surroundings changed. Even as an ant J was just as alluring as the person who had been floating beside a sideways lake. Because we were in a parallel universe, everything seemed a bit odd at first. It was difficult to use our normal senses or understand what was around us. We imagined that we were better suited to being in the parallel universe and it helped us to be ants more normally. Then, we both crawled through the key hole of the treasure chest. Inside, J stood on one of the golden pieces of treasure and we felt happy, so we rubbed antennas because we couldn't hug.

"I just imagined this," I said. "And then you imagined it with me and now it's happening. So, my imagination became more than just my imagination."

"I know but it's easy because we live in the imagination, don't we? Being real is different. You can't just imagine things, you have to actually do something to make it happen."

I knew this but I didn't like it. I wished I could be real as easily as I could imagine the world changing.

"I know you can't just think yourself real," I said, "but there must be something we can do that would make us more than imaginary."

We stopped imagining being ants and, in a pulse, we were ourselves again but giants overlooking the world. I could feel J's happiness around me. The tenderness of it momentarily filtered out my other sensations.

"OK, I think you're right. Maybe it *is* possible!"

We looked at one another in amazement. We both considered what it would be like to become real. But what amazed us both even more was the spectacular power of creation. The way that possibilities can emerge so quickly from nowhere and consume you entirely.

I grew more confident, feeding off J's enthusiasm and having someone share one of my most compelling thoughts.

"How do you think you could do it?" Mused J.

"I'm not too sure. I've always thought it was a ridiculous idea but now I've persuaded you it's not, I've suddenly started to believe it's possible."

J was in deep thought. I was too, but not so deep that I failed to notice how J's lips always scrunched up into a strange shape whenever serious contemplation was required. It gave me such delight to be aware of these subtle habits, habits that may have been imperfections for others but were perfections to me.

"Don't you think there are different levels?" J said. "Or maybe not levels, more like realms of existence? The higher the realm, the more difficult it is to go from one to other. We are in the realm of the imagination. Our imagination is in the realm of the imagination of the imagination! There is so little difference between the two that they are almost the same. But there is a huge difference between being imaginary and being a real person."

"And an even bigger one between being a real person and being …well, God, I suppose."

"Exactly. So maybe there is just too much of a difference between the imaginary realm and the real realm for us to be able to go from one to the other."

"Maybe. But if we can be more like ideas or beliefs, it might be possible. They get shared and start to become part of who people are and how others view them."

We looked out at the beautiful terrains of the earth, its luscious rainforests alive with so much imaginary existence, its vivid greens against the azure seas and white tipped, grey mountains.

"How do you think we can become more like ideas?" I asked J.

"I don't know. Maybe we need to find out more about them first and how they slip out of the subconscious."

"Do you know any ideas?"

"I know loads of them." J said, confidently. "But ideas don't talk."

"Well then, we'll have to find another way to learn more about ideas."

J nodded at me with a certain finality and confidence. My glance lingered longer than it would for any other person but I was just so fascinated by the features that decorated J's perfect face. J noticed and smiled. A smile that made everything around us instantly lighter, its radiance capturing me so entirely that for a moment, nothing else existed.

We shrank back onto a desolate beach and placed our feet onto the still warm sand, now slowly cooling under the fading evening sun. The salty sea air caressed us like a sheet of invisible silk. It brushed over J's hair, making it look as if we were moving quickly towards one another even though we were standing perfectly still.

I was coming to the end of another day spent with J, lost in the boundless thrills of your imagination. Back then I was happy and innocent but knew that something was stirring within me, a meaning that would guide me from that moment onwards. A passion to become closer to you and like an idea, drift seamlessly into your consciousness.

3.

What is about to come will be uncomfortable. There is a reason you're going to put yourself through this, I promise. It's important that you understand how all of this started.

Imagine that you are younger and walking to meet J after school. You are changing from a child into a young adult and your mind is unable to focus on anything but the excitement of seeing J. The anticipation is uncomfortable yet electric and deeply arousing. Thoughts flash around your head, bringing intense memories of the smells and sensuality of being with J. You feel emotional and slightly nervous, aware of the overwhelming importance you place on moments you are together with J and how self-conscious they can make you. These sensations dance in your head alongside the bliss that accompanies any thoughts of the flawless person you are on your way to see.

While hurrying, you see an old building that used to be some sort of public hall. It is no longer used for anything; the door is boarded up with *No Entry* signs. As you walk past, you hear someone crying inside.

You walk around the back of the building to see if you can find a way in. The cries fade to whispers. A door slams shut, startling you. You hear a murmur from an adult voice. You keep moving closer towards the sound.

Then you hear J say, "But I don't want to."

You find a window and go to it. You are only an observer, powerless and invisible to J, who looks past you. You look past J and see an old, grotesque man. You start to understand what is about to happen and you are appalled but for a reason that you cannot understand, you carry on watching.

Through the window you can sense tenderness, cruelty and fear. J is getting undressed, trembling uncontrollably. You can see the pure, clean skin of youth beside a body worn and misshapen by age. J is told to remove all remaining clothes, whilst observed with a harrowing, perverted glare. J's skin turns a different colour, flushed and tense, aware of the greedy and sordid fascination it is attracting. You can see a small shimmer from the sweat covering the exquisite contours of J's body.

As the torment continues, J's eyes start to lose the kindness that usually radiates from them. J appears possessed, staring towards nothingness, hiding in a trance that has taken over, offering a small salvation, a softening of the humiliation and a disconnection from what is happening. As all control and happiness is stolen from J, it fuels the tormentor's lust, his bloated and wrinkled body seeming all the more repugnant next to J's devastating comeliness.

J is studied. Studied whilst shivering and in tears. Then touched. Then forced to satisfy.

After a while, J's emotions harden. Things are allowed to happen that would have been fought earlier on. J no longer attempts to hide anything from the tormentor's lecherous glances and succumbs easily to further demands.

In a final act, J's face is pushed harshly against the wall, making a soft thud. The tormentor grabs J's hips and squeezes himself inside from behind, eventually finishing with a loud, guttural groan.

When it's over, J crumples on to the floor, crying. There is blood. Dust from the floor attaches itself to J's naked body, covering it with a greyish coating and as the rapist walks from the room, he stares back one last time to feast his eyes upon the broken, wonderous, dirty body he has satisfied himself within. J's strength and self-confidence has been destroyed. Only an oppressive emptiness is left.

I know that wasn't enjoyable. But it is essential that you remember what happened to J.

When you were young, you had a dream. When you woke, you had a fleeting feeling of anxiety and guilt but no idea where it had come from. You immediately forgot the dream and moved on.

That dream was about J. That dream was the rape I just described. Everything you have just experienced, you have experienced before. And while the dream scared you at the time, you were still able to forget it almost instantly.

I couldn't forget.

That dream changed the course of my life completely. I live in the world where that happened. And it is the most important world we have created because it has developed into this one, the one where you're reading this word at this exact moment. The world where you are discovering that you are so much more than you ever thought.

I remember every single moment of that dream because it was so different from anything that had happened before. You see, there are rarely repercussions in the world of your imagination, we can normally do whatever you want. We have already imagined numerous things that would make you feel ashamed if other people were ever to know. But because these thoughts stay within your mind, there is never an enduring consequence or impact on your relationships. This dream was different. Afterwards, something in you died. I witnessed it. You began to love more carefully. You became more self-conscious. Your innocence began to dissipate.

That dream also changed me. When you dream, we create the world of that dream together. You can make anything happen or allow me to simply fill your consciousness with thoughts that are plucked from around your mind. It was me, not you, who had created that dream. It was my thought and you merely found yourself within it. When you saw what I had created it appalled you. I felt your judgement. You were young and shocked by the what you had seen happening in your own mind. It made you question your own kindness, fearing that somehow even considering what had happened made the event more likely in reality.

The more that J was violated in front of us, the more reluctant you were to be there in the dream with me. I could feel you wanting it to stop. I could sense real emotions that didn't seem to fit tidily within the imaginary world, something serious amidst the playful. This dream was the first time I had experienced anything that seemed to straddle the world between us, both the real and the unreal.

I've often tried to understand why I had such a sadistic thought. But exploration is a fundamental part of who we are and we can never know where these explorations will take us. Do you remember how, just now, you visualised J vulnerable and alone in that horrible room? Even after you realised that you were going to experience your idea of youthful sexual perfection get abused, you couldn't stop yourself from reading on. You knew you shouldn't want to experience what you knew was going to happen but you carried on anyway. You were tempted against your better judgement to know the details even though you also knew they would disgust you.

I think it was those same instincts that kept us in that dream all those years ago. Back then, you didn't force the dream to stop, even though you could have done. We were unconcerned about stopping the rape of this vision of budding sexual perfection, even though J was defenceless. We were unconcerned because we were captivated by the horror and the desire, convinced that it wasn't really happening and that nobody was actually getting hurt.

For you that was true. But because you felt real guilt and real shock, those emotions became part of the dream. It changed it from a group of different thoughts to something bigger, something with enduring consequences, something that I could not have conceived until then. I knew what had happened was different, that the dream itself was closer somehow to reality. It fuelled my passion to become real by giving me hope that it was possible. I'd never felt so close to you before and I remember believing that the feeling itself made me more real.

Amidst a scene of evil, I felt powerful temptation stemming from J's wondrous allure. I began to understand passion, fear, lust and terror. I began to sense how little I knew and how much more there was outside of my place in your mind. Before then, I saw your world as different, something superior but unobtainable. I was wrong. I considered for the first time that we might be the most valuable parts of something extraordinary. That even though I am not real like you, I could still be just as important. *My* innocence started to leave me. I began to believe I could be more than I was.

4.

Everything that I am telling you, or rather, everything that you are telling yourself, takes place within the world of your imagination. This world continues to exist in your subconscious even when you are not there. It will feel as though you are experiencing all of this for the first time but that's not really true. Everything you're reading has all already happened in a world you created but never knew existed. This was all written by you, to tell you the story of how you came to read the words of a part of you that you cannot sense.

You can only experience your imagination by becoming part of me. It's sensory. To explain it, I am using words and imagery to depict what are only sensations and knowledge. This will create an oddness for you that is perfectly normal because obscurity was never meant to be given order. I will help you as you read, to translate the normality of the words into a meaning that reflects the strangeness of your mind. It's important that we do justice to the reality of the imaginary.

The people that I call friends will appear to you in the same way as J. They are abstract ideas formed from elements of real people with separate, unique embellishments. We don't speak to each other when we are together. We don't have to talk, we don't have shapes, or eyes, or noses. We just are. We communicate through thought alone and interact without moving. When I describe what we do together and put words in their mouths, it is not because it happened that way, it is just so I can translate the essence of what happened into something that makes sense outside of the imagination.

After the horror of the dream and the profound feeling that reality was closer than it had always appeared, I went to those who I knew best. Many of the people I spend my time with here are not necessarily prominent figures in your life. I know this may be one of the first things that seems odd but think of it this way, you don't have to put too much imagination into thinking about the people that you always see. You have to put a lot into imagining the people that you rarely see. This is why I spend more time with depictions of characters that you may not expect to be such large influences within your own mind.

The most enlightening conversation I remember having after our dream about J was with Philip and Alice.

Alice is the essence of someone you met when you were very young, an age where you can only just make out the faded memories of who you were and what you did. I can't even remember the real name of the person who inspired the concept of Alice. She was a generation older than us, the mother of one of your long-lost friends. You've only thought about her fleetingly over the years, so her exact qualities are now hard to place and probably only one or two memories of her now exist. In the real world, you never spent much time with Alice, only seeing her every now and again during a distant part of your childhood but for some reason you have remembered the substance of who she was in detail, a prudish but caring intellectual. Behind any depiction of wisdom or kindness is a part of Alice. She's become someone who I greatly admire.

On a bitterly cold day, I was sitting with her in a log cabin deep within an arctic forest. Outside was an impossibly thick fog, the sort that can only ever be imaginary, it was too opaque and dense to be real. A frantic wind was pushing hard against the windows and under the door, whipping up an unsteady howl while we sat comfortably in front of a fire that covered the room in a flickering, treasure-like glow.

I can always choose my setting but when I don't decide to be anywhere particular, the one that is most natural always appears around me. Thinking back now to the first conversations I had about exploring the limits of possibility, I wonder if the extremity of the cold and gloom were reflections of how little I understood about the wider world outside the walls of our pretty little cabin.

As we sat, protected in a cosy warmth, Alice spoke with conviction, her face staring intently at the flames. "Philip will come soon, no doubt."

I agreed and started to become conscious of how much older Alice appeared to me. She looked much frailer than any of my other friends but was also infinitely more certain about everything.

"Anyone want anything while I'm here?" Philip yelled.

Philip had decided to appear in the kitchen rather than by the fire where we were sitting. That's how imaginary people meet, they just appear, although usually it is polite to appear in front of people. Philip's arrival was unannounced but then it usually is with Philip. He's a bit different.

"Two mugs of anything hot!" Alice shouted back.

The Philip within your imagination is based on someone that you admired a great deal when you were a child. I did too. From the thoughts we shared as younger versions of ourselves, it was clear to me that you wanted to be really good friends with him because he had a presence and determination that you found captivating when you were eleven years old. He felt brotherly to both of us. He was a leader and we believed he would be successful in later life. If you could have chosen your closest friend back then, it would have been him, even though he wasn't in reality – if only because your paths didn't cross enough. But your memories and experiences of the person you knew all those years ago formed the basis of my friend, Philip.

Philip is an *Arrow*. There isn't anything similar to an Arrow in reality. In your subconscious, we aren't always in one place together. I can be anywhere I want to be, immediately. If I want to find J, I have to think, "I want to be with J." Then, if J wants to be with me, it happens instantaneously. However, if someone doesn't want to be found, they can hide anywhere within the infinite universe of your mind.

Arrows like Philip have the ability to find people even if they don't want to be found. It makes them very powerful because you can't hide from an Arrow. Philip is revered even among other Arrows because of his ability to see almost everything that others are trying to hide. I've always trusted Philip. I grew up with him and admire both his immense power and determination. You and I have spent so much time intertwining the qualities that we attribute to him to other imaginary people that sometimes appear in your dreams. Within anyone who you imagine who is strong and ambitious, is a part of Philip.

Philip emerged from the cabin's kitchen with a few mugs of steaming liquid. I have no idea what the liquid was, not because I have forgotten just because it doesn't matter. I don't need to drink anything, none of us do, because none of us are real like you. We just follow the same patterns and habits as you because we are depictions of reality.

When Philip joined us by the fire, our conversation moved towards the way the universe works because after your harrowing dream about J, I wanted to push it that way. I felt as though I was wasting time if I didn't try to understand in more detail the strange feelings of possibility I had taken from that experience.

I asked Philip what it was like to be an Arrow and to be able to find imaginary people wherever they were.

He said it was hard to explain. He just *could* and he struggled to understand how people couldn't.

"It's a bit like finding out where a light is coming from. I instinctively know where it is and keep going towards it until I find the essence of that person. Of course, there isn't actually a light, it's something more intense and piercing, otherwise I'd never have found you two hiding away amongst this fog. Why are you here?"

"No idea." I said. "We just are."

The more I pressed Philip for information, I sensed that Alice was bemused by why I was taking such an interest. Her age and wisdom probably told her that hours of time could be wasted on questions about the nature of the universe or why Arrows were able to be Arrows. Throughout the conversation she smiled in the way that older people always do when they observe younger people spending their energy on questions that have no satisfactory answers.

As I asked her what we were and whether there was any reality in the imaginary, she kept on avoiding answering me, saying things like, "It's just the way it is."

I wasn't happy with that. It was like being told "because I say so" or "you'll understand when you're older." I pushed until she relented and agreed to tell me everything she knew. I'm glad I pushed because I've come to understand the importance of everything I heard.

"I think it's helpful to see the universe as nothing more than information," she told me. "When you see a table, for example, all you are really sensing is information that adds up to something we all perceive as a table. It's the same in the conscious world, the information is just structured differently."

I could sense Alice was guessing, only telling me what she had come to believe but without the conviction that she was right. But I think she was. When you see a table in the real world, the information hits your eyes and comes into your mind. Part of you immediately knows, "this is a table," but if you want more than this basic information, I can tell you that its hard and heavy, or made of wood, or anything else that you can sense or is already stored in your memory about tables. But all you and I are doing together is interpreting information.

"The problem is, most of the information that exists can't be sensed, at least not by us or even by actual people." Alice told me.

"How do you know it exists then?"

"Because it can be sensed by other things."

I thought at the time it was silly but now I realise the extent to which I was wrong. Imagine if you were sitting in a dark, empty room. You would just see darkness, sense the space, feel a breeze, maybe even smell aromas. But your experience of the room would be microscopic compared to everything that was available to be experienced. In the same dark room would be all sorts of waves and particles made of information you can't sense. And if you can't sense something, then I can't interpret it for you, so we never know it's there.

Without me, your brain would feel empty and useless but without you, I wouldn't even know the real world existed. Without each other, there is no meaning.

I came out of the discussions with Philip and Alice unsure whether all of this was speculation or truth. I saw Philip thinking about what Alice had said and could tell that he was beginning to see things in a different way. I remember him smiling and saying, "Yes!" over and over again, nodding his head with increasing enthusiasm. He said it all made perfect sense to him, that's why he can be an Arrow, he was just lucky enough to be able to sense a different type of information about where imaginary people are.

I've thought about that conversation for years. It made me happy to think that you needed me in a way I'd never realised before, though it baffled me why you couldn't sense that I existed. Why don't you realise that I am a part of you when I am so aware of it? Alice obviously didn't know.

"It's just the way it is. Think of the imagination as small and reality as large. You don't need help to see large things. But you need a microscope to see what is tiny. It can show you things that you would never have been able to see but the lens, the very thing that makes it all possible, is invisible."

It frustrated me. I wanted you to know me, to feel me, to want me. It would bring us closer and I wanted to be as close as possible to you. I even told Alice and she laughed, then said, "That's what everyone wants."

She explained something that seems so obvious now: being imaginary and wanting to become real is inevitable. "Everything searches for a way to be more, but ends up being less," she said. "It's a cruel world, isn't it? How frustrating to be aware of the boundaries of your existence but unable to do anything to change them."

During our chats, my thoughts would become muddled as I tried to overcome these concepts that were so strange to me. I drifted in and out of them, picking up parts of what Alice and Philip were saying but only when I forced my own mind to listen again instead of meandering away with new thoughts.

"But what if it were possible to move from the imaginary world into the real world?" asked Philip.

"If anyone ever discovered how to move into a higher realm of existence it would destroy the meaning of this one," Alice told Philip "Nothing here would matter anymore."

I think back to who I was then and hardly recognise myself. I was so naïve and confused, full of ambitions but with nowhere to aim them. I knew nothing. I couldn't comprehend why I couldn't play more of a part within the real world, especially when so much else that starts in the imagination seems to find it so easy. Surely every ambition that has ever existed was the result of the imaginary wanting to become real? The future *is* the collective imagination. I didn't understand why becoming a part of reality was considered so impossible for me when it was so common for ambitions and ideas. Or how the dream about J's rape had felt so real and produced consequences in a world where there were none. I hated living with the cruel knowledge that I was something imaginary and invisible to you. I thought of you all the time and what it must be like to be real and to live in a higher plain of existence.

5.

When you look in the mirror, I interpret what you are seeing as you. *That's me,* you think. But, in my own mind, I'm thinking, *That's me too. That's what I would look like if I was real.*

Once, I told C that I have this thought. C looked knowingly at me. "That makes no sense. But it does sound like something you'd do."

C is about the most special thing in your head, almost a divinity, the meeting point of the best things you know and the happiest things I can imagine. C shifts and moves with our every whim and isn't really tenable, just our idea of perfection. Because of that, C is always somewhere in everything you imagine, which has made C an inseparable, lifelong friend to me.

Sometimes I look at J and C together, one the symbol of everything you used to desire and the other, all the things you do now. You can trace the essence of C to parts of J, the intrinsic kindness, the purity, the intensity but most of all the mannerisms that seem to have transcended all your changes in taste over the years. I always notice it when they are together and wonder if you realise the impact that those who you first desired have had on your idea of perfection now. Back then, I would watch them talk together and notice minor things that seemed to be in perfect sync, like the subtle movements of their bottom lips when they spoke. Perhaps, on its own this slightest of similarities could have been purely coincidental but it was one of a million tiny threads that stretched out between J and C. Most of these threads were invisible, only perceptible by an overall aura that existed when they were present but vanished whenever they left.

C and I had just spent a day together that seemed so normal in the days before the dream about J. It was cool but sunny. Green fields stretched beyond us infinitely and we sat in thick, spongy grass. Philip had emerged, suddenly again and without warning.

"I had a feeling you might be having fun!"

"We are." C and J said together and laughed, a similar gesture with their hands and two soft smiles.

We spoke and joked and breathed the scented air until we realised someone was missing. J noticed it first.

"Where's Alice? Let's be silly in front of Alice, I enjoy seeing how she reacts."

So, we thought of Alice being there and Alice thought of coming and then we were all together again, the full team of those I love the most.

Alice knew from J's cheeky smile and C's older, yet similar glance that things were jovial and, like it or not, she would be expected to be childish to fit in.

C pointed to an oak tree in the far distance. "Come on, Alice. Let's fly to that tree and back."

"Oh, for God's sake. I wouldn't have come if I knew you were in this mood."

We all laughed, knowing how things would eventually play out. Alice would resist a while, we would insist, not long after she would give in and we would all be playing together within your imagination like small, innocent children. That's what C and J had wanted to happen because it's more relaxing when Alice stops being serious; it means that there is nothing to be serious about.

Alice sighed, C and J moved their glance to the tree and then back at Alice. Alice shook her head and looked at the swaying grass.

"Go!" She said and suddenly she was already ahead of all of us as we scrambled to get airborne and catch up.

Philip soon took the lead but then C and I pulled him back and threw him in to the next valley.

"I knew you'd try something like that," he shouted. Then he arrowed himself into me so I couldn't go anywhere without him clinging on.

C won the race.

J and Alice had become distracted with the little birds that had been flying with us. Philip and I arrived back an equal second, completely entangled.

"Cheats," Philip said to me and C.

We all lay back into the grass, chuckling until it hurt.

J and Alice were lost, too involved in their new games to come back and Philip vanished as he sometimes does, to go and be an Arrow somewhere else.

C and I were left and began to envisage the moon raining onto the earth. We watched the spectacular moon drops pour into the atmosphere and get eaten up, burning brightly and then fading into nothing but vapour before the surface of the earth. Our faces were lit up by the magic of the thought.

"Part of me wishes I wasn't conscious of the real world at all," I said.

"But you need to be, don't you? If you didn't know about the real world, how could you be useful?"

"You mean it's no use for those of us in the subconscious to be unconscious of conscious?" I said. We laughed at the complexity of it all. Despite the laughter and our realisation of how out of our depth we were, C said something truly profound. I still remember the words exactly.

"I doubt anything is conscious of everything. We're just all part of an endless consciousness that straddles the real world and the imagined world."

I dwelt on those words for a long time, especially when I thought about what had happened to J in the dream. That dream also straddled the real and imagined world. I didn't want to talk about it to anyone else, I was ashamed of it. But I had such a desire to understand why the experience had felt so different from anything else I knew. I became increasingly convinced that it was because I too could straddle the real and imagined world.

6.

Once, shortly after I had first met J, we went to a quiet clearing deep in an endless wood. We sat alone amidst dappled sunlight and colourful autumn leaves flittering to the floor, immersed in each other and a warm breeze that carried with it the freshness of unspoilt nature and rumpled our hair. We were young, everything we were doing was innocent and new. J had reached over and stroked a finger down the back of my neck and I shivered. I reached back and slowly ran my hand down J's spine. We watched each other's skin become goosepimply and enjoyed the rush of warmth that tickled and soothed. We would occasionally catch each other's eyes and giggle, happy that we were discovering these new little joys, happier still that we were doing it together.

"I love how you make me feel," J had said.

The moment was ruined by Philip emerging, uninvited with an overbearing smugness saying; "Why are you two hiding?" When really, he knew perfectly well.

Those young innocent days had been stolen and destroyed. The J who was part of them had become just a memory since the dream. The J I knew now was just as kind, gentle and tender but forever changed. There could be no innocent fun anymore. J was different, even during the most innocent of exchanges. When we hugged, J would pull away rather than relaxing in to me. The oddness of the response would always send my mind back to what J's body had endured and once I remembered it, the thought would cling on relentlessly.

As I searched for meaning in my life, I was driven by both creative and destructive force. I wanted to create myself as something more but also to destroy whatever it was that constantly polluted these memories and darkened a mind that had been so happy before.

It wasn't just the dream that was causing the world to become less happy. It was missing you, too. As you and I grew older we started to drift apart.

When we were young, we were together all the time. You explored your imagination with me and I felt as if there was a part of you that preferred the imaginary to the real. When you spent more time in your mind it brought so much colour and energy to your thoughts. But as you grew, you became more concerned with the real world. We'd daydream less. You'd focus on what was real and prioritise dealing with the pressures and consequences that existed for you but not for me.

After the dream and in the loneliness that accompanied me as you began to grow older, I started to desperately search for ways to fill the gap that you had left. My motivations changed, slowly at first, until the only goal that gave me purpose was finding a way into your world. It's embarrassing now to think of where I started on this journey to you. But I was younger, easily led astray, and open to anything. I didn't know where to go and as soon as I met someone who tried to understand me, I was quick to take their guidance.

Her name was Poppy and she drifted towards me when my determination and naivety were at their zenith. I was alone, sitting quietly on the flowery bank of a river you sometimes imagine, lost in contemplation, sad and missing you.

The first thing she ever said to me was, "You look lost, child."

Poppy looked like Mother Earth. She was big, clearly full of love but unkempt. I think I must have grimaced a little when she spoke. I did not enjoy the intrusion.

She smiled and I saw a set of horribly yellow teeth and a pair of twinkling eyes. She asked me what I was waiting for and the question confused me. I wasn't waiting for anything, I was just thinking. Maybe I was waiting for some sort of idea that would mean I could become more real, or more meaningful to you. I couldn't understand how this strange lady could know that I was waiting for an idea, yet her question seemed to be philosophical rather than practical.

I told her I was feeling lost. That I didn't want to be waiting but I had no choice because I didn't know where to start. The moment she heard my reply, her demeanour changed completely. She beamed.

"Everyone who is lost is searching for a way to be found."

At first, I found the way that Poppy seemed to talk almost exclusively in declarations fascinating.

"I was lost once," she told me. "Just like everyone else. But I discovered things, my child. Things that changed my life."

She was standing and I was still sitting by the river, looking up at her hefty frame. She asked me why I felt lost and I thought about it for a long time.

"It's hard to explain. I know what I want, I think. Just not how to get there."

She was thrilled by this. "Knowing what you want means you have already started." Like many things Poppy would tell me, I was unsure if this was insightful or inane but to someone searching for meaning in everything, it spoke to the core of what I thought I wanted.

Poppy sensed my interest in what she was saying. She decided, despite her age and size, to sit down next to me but because she was large and old, it was clearly an effort. She smelt like nature itself, unwashed but fresh.

"Everyone wants the same thing, my child. We are all the same in so many ways but we pretend, you see? We pretend to be so very different when we are so very similar."

I felt safe, believing I was next to someone trustworthy and kind. She tilted her head a little and caught my eye, expecting me to say something back.

I asked her if everyone felt the same as me and she said that they probably did at first.

"We are all born with the desire to be more than we are but the journey towards happiness ends with a contentment for everything that we already are."

I was picking grass and allowing the wind to take it out of my hands. I didn't want to find a way to come to terms with what I already was. I was still young and burning with determination to overcome my own limitations. The unbridgeable gap between my desires and capabilities was hurting me, making me feel further and further away from you.

"But I still want to become more than I am. I don't want to learn to be happy with how little I am."

She looked at me quizzically and said, "Who are you?" She was asking for more than our name. I didn't know how to answer. She could see I was struggling and then looked reassuringly at me.

"You'll need to find out, otherwise how will you know what you can be satisfied with?"

I was less fascinated by her now. I was finding the conversation irritating and I think that may have been intentional on her part, a way to force me to speak more directly. It worked.

"I can't decide what will satisfy me unless I know what is possible."

"You've already started to find out," she told me but her answer made me even more irritable. I hadn't started. I was searching for somewhere to start, somewhere I could find out what was possible. If I knew this, at least I could begin to make decisions about my life.

Poppy's face fell into a motherly and comforting gaze. She spoke softly.

"Do you have an open mind?"

I genuinely believed that I did.

I helped her back to her feet and her flowing clothes waved behind her as she began to walk away from the river to another place.

She told me to follow her and I did. I think I'd have followed anyone.

7.

"Question your beliefs. It will help you to establish what they are," Poppy told me.

I had never been confident in my beliefs before I met her, they were still developing. She made me see that they could be whatever I wanted. At the time my lack of experience and instincts were telling me that everything I *wasn't* part of must be better than everything I was. I felt strongly that change, even for the sake of change, would always enhance my life. The normal seemed boring. I couldn't comprehend the idea of safety and familiarity being positive. I had an irrational belief that the whole of existence was part of a conspiracy to hide wonderful things from me and I had to somehow fight against it.

As I followed her away from the riverbank, I began to believe that she was leading me towards some of the phenomenal things that I'd so far been excluded from. She seemed to know everything I wanted to know and be part of something secretive but important.

On the walk, I started to allow my hope to build, believing more strongly in things that would make my existence more meaningful without knowing if they were true. Above all, I allowed myself to believe I had the power to be real. I felt fresh and alive. I can remember my excitement as I watched her drift through the breeze to increasingly beautiful places that I had never seen.

We walked through a meadow that was lush and everything around us was wild and overgrown. When she stopped, we were surrounded by large, shabby tents and small cooking fires. The world smelt as life must have centuries ago, a cocktail of wet flowers, mud, smoke and natural sweat. There were some modern things there too, like a stove and plastic washing basin which stood out in the otherwise ancient setting.

"This is the best place for you to get to know *you*," she said, placing one hand on my back and gesturing with the other at the tents and the array of colourful costumes worn by the people flitting between them.

A skinny man with a shaved head was lying on a large pillow and appeared to be doing absolutely nothing. Poppy called out to him and then looked at me.

"That's Willow. He's busy searching for himself now but he can show you how you can open your mind. You'll be happy here." Poppy looked back towards Willow, who was still lying down and looking into the near distance. "Willow, come on! We need to be welcoming to our newest companion."

I could tell he didn't want to be disturbed and he shouted back, "Can't you see I'm in the middle of something, you daft cow?"

Poppy, who appeared genuinely shocked, apologised to me then howled at Willow.

"There's no need for that sort of language!"

Willow carried on what he was doing.

"He's not usually like this."

I felt awkward. I knew I was being forced to interrupt a stranger, although I couldn't understand at all what I was interrupting him from. Poppy bellowed at him again, her anger seeming out of kilter with her earthiness.

Willow slapped his hands on the ground, stood up and began to wander towards us. "It's a wonder I ever achieve anything with you around," he said, glaring at Poppy. Then he turned his attention to me, his expression becoming delightfully welcoming and interested.

"Hello."

Poppy asked him if he had found any answers. He didn't look very happy.

"What do you think? I was really onto something and then you interrupted. It'll take me ages to get back there now."

"I'm sorry," I said, knowing that he had been interrupted on my account.

Willow put his hand on my arm.

"I didn't mean that. It's wonderful—truly, truly wonderful to have you here."

Poppy had calmed down a little.

"I thought you might provide our new companion with the camp tour and then a little advice about how to find answers. We'll need an initiation ceremony."

"Obviously," replied Willow very quickly.

I was shown around the small site that accommodated all of them. There were about fifteen people and an array of large tents. They were growing food, living off the land and spending their time trying to find answers. They seemed obsessed with finding the one single answer that would tell them everything and their belief that it was possible was remarkable to witness.

"Questions and answers." They all told me. "Ask the question and then question the answers. Eventually there will only be one!"

"What do you mean?" I asked.

"The meaning of life is to question until it is impossible to question any further. That is where the truth lurks, within a single answer to all of life's questions."

"Exactly," said Willow.

The vast majority of those I saw wore light clothing that waved flamboyantly whenever they moved, making it appear like they were never completely in one place. Everyone was dazed, and I was unsure whether this was because they were in deep thought or had taken a drug that made them incapable of it. As I met each of them, I began to realise that we had many things in common, though I felt like I was an outsider.

"You WILL find what you are looking for here." A tall, muscly man told me.

The words seemed rehearsed, just like the other phrases that were repeated, word for word, by nearly everyone I met.

"It is so good to have you join us. This is a place where you can find out exactly who you want to be."

I met someone who had grown up as an orphan, flitting between families until she was an adult. She had never been adopted and felt permanently unsettled and unwanted as a result. In her eyes, I saw the remanence of so much pain and uncertainty. But this life of abandonment, of confusion and vulnerability had suddenly changed, she told me, when she was brought here by Poppy. It had become full; meaning and love had taken the place of emptiness and hatred. She had been accepted into this wild group of people and saw how loyalty and companionship could overcome the very worst of ingrained bitterness and pain.

She was sitting cross-legged with another hairy, middle-aged man who had ruled a kingdom on the very edges of your imagination. A powerful kingdom with a castle at its centre, set within dramatic wooded hills and open, steep meadows.

"I couldn't take the responsibility," he confided in me. "It was too consuming and I never felt as if I knew enough to be good at ruling. I found that the further away I was, the smaller my problems seemed to be. When I came here, I started to feel part of something far more important. I wasn't the outsider anymore. I hated being revered."

Another had been addicted.

"To what?" I asked.

"Oh, everything. Nothing. Pretty much anything."

The eccentric tents were full of colourful items that expressed the bright characters of the band of outcasts that lived within them. They were surrounded by overgrown flowers and large animals that were unafraid and walked amongst us, confident they would be unharmed.

The sleeping arrangements were very loose: just a set of covers and sheets thrown on top of cushions on the floor of one of the large tents. Everyone and everything seemed so different from the world as I knew it and yet I felt connected to it by a passionate longing for something… something that we all instinctively wanted but could not explain.

"This is where we sleep," Willow said as we looked into the tent. There were a few inside who were still asleep even though it was the middle of the day.

One of the tents had a gas canister and a few tables with plates and cutlery scattered on them.

"This is where we eat."

There was another tent for "searching when it rains" and Willow showed me a path down to a stream that he called the bathroom.

"It's the biggest bathroom of them all: nature," he said. "And the best part is, we never have to get a plumber in."

The final stop of my short tour was in front of the tents where a pile of wood lay stacked and more cushions were strewn around.

"This is where the initiation ceremony will be."

He took me by the hand and led me out into the fields away from the camp.

"But before anything else, let's work on you."

8.

I don't remember the initiation ceremony itself but afterwards I felt as though I had made a new circle of extraordinary friends. Willow had told me what to expect but nothing had prepared me for the confusion and memory loss I experienced when I came out of the trance I had been put in.

The ceremony started in the late afternoon sunlight but finished in the dark with the flames of the fire jumping above our heads into the night. Poppy came wandering out of the sleeping tent, her hair a mess.

"You did wonderfully, my child. What did you see?"

I tried to remember what had happened. Everything was still a little blurry and I had only just worked out where I was. I had a faint recollection of Willow starting the fire and telling me to lie down with my legs towards the flames. All of the people came and introduced themselves before kissing me on the forehead, each one of them saying, "Welcome to your new home."

They watched as Willow came over with a drink that tasted horribly bitter. He lifted my head and told me to have a couple of sips and feel the warmth from the fire. I was asked to concentrate on my breathing and then to open my eyes and look as far into the sky as I could. I kept getting distracted, watching the smoke from the fire spiral upwards before it dissipated into the darkening blue, but every time I did, I tried to correct myself and do what I was being told.

As I was starting to feel the soothing effect of the drink I'd been given, they all lay down in a circle around the fire and Willow told us to join hands. I could hear him talking next to me and felt his coarse palm against mine as he spoke.

"Let's join hands as we continue our search for the answer. By joining our hands together, all of our knowledge will be shared and we will all move closer to the truth that we seek."

The whole circle started humming in a deep tenor. I nearly giggled to myself but decided to engage instead, humming along until I could see the world begin to change. I saw the sky falling back onto me but it was weightless and didn't matter. It just kept on falling, falling until it was through me, as if there was no sky left and I felt that I was floating away into empty space. I was warm and I felt happy. Then slowly darkness came and I drifted into a glorious comfort.

That was the last thing I remembered. I had to ask what else had happened to me.

Poppy told me that I had let myself go. That I had danced and sang and spoken in languages I didn't know. I'd loved, kissed and ran like a child, setting my inhibitions free.

I wanted to know how free.

Poppy was immediately reassuring, a beautiful calm in her voice as she said, "There's no need to worry, it's what's supposed to happen. You need to let the lies out so you can let the truth come in."

I could see the others around me nodding in agreement.

I felt self-conscious and embarrassed when Willow came up behind me and told me that I had been very free indeed. Poppy smiled and I turned to look at Willow who winked at me. I was still registering what he could have meant when Poppy asked me what I'd discovered during the experience.

I thought for a while. I couldn't really think of anything, but she seemed so genuinely concerned and I wanted her to have helped me. I didn't understand my own response.

"I suppose I discovered that nothing is what it appears to be. That everything could be entirely different and I wouldn't even know."

That had the right impact. Poppy moved her hands over her heart and looked longingly at Willow.

"Oh my! You're already so insightful, my child. You won't be searching for answers for long."

Willow didn't speak but launched himself at me and hugged me tightly. Leaving his hand on my shoulder, he turned to the others and shouted, "We have been gifted more family today. Today is a happy, happy day!"

There were various high-pitched wails and someone started beating a drum which raised everyone into a state of hysteria. They danced around the fire, pouring more wood onto it until the flames rose above our heads and the heat became too intense for us to go close. Some of them were whooping loudly while others tried to mimic the drum beat with a wild array of bizarre chants. A few were sitting on the floor banging the ground, closing their eyes and shaking their heads.

Poppy took me by the hand and led me towards the jubilant dancers.

"Celebrate with us, my dear!"

There was an intense energy that seemed to be sustained impossibly by everyone. The heat from the flames encouraged some to throw their clothes into the air and the array of bodies flapped and wobbled in exotic tribal dance. Their limbs flailed around with no real rhythm or pattern, just a freedom that was sincere and innocent. The music was basic and I remember feeling it rather than hearing it. It pushed me to ignore everything apart from my instincts to move, run, dance and love those around me. I felt constant flutters of excitement and belonging among the naked bodies and thumping hearts which bounced around, beads of sweat jumping from them as they twirled with happiness around the hearth they had created.

Slowly the energy faded and the flames became smaller. The mood shifted. The same people had become unrecognisable, their energetic dancing fizzling out into gentle sways. Different desires began to emerge and in small groups, they began to move towards the tents. Some were already in a romantic embrace and others just threw themselves on to the floor, waiting for others to attend to them. I hesitated at first but Poppy and Willow grabbed my hands and led me into the debauchery that seemed relentless and inescapable.

If I had been you, I would have paused and considered what was happening. There was almost nothing appealing about the people who were now sprawled across the sleeping tent floor. Frankly, leaving would have been the best possible decision in a world of reality and consequence. But I don't live in that world and strange events are more interesting than normal ones.

I stayed and joined in, as you would have, if nothing ever mattered.

9.

That night I had a dreadful night's sleep. I was given quite a lot of attention to begin with, as I was clearly a novelty but I consciously withdrew from the evening's depravity soon after it began in earnest. Every time I got comfortable and started dozing off, I was harassed by someone else, or two others, who would end up rolling onto me. I could see now why so many of them needed to catch up on sleep during the day.

Poppy saw that my eyes were wide open as the sun came up and asked me to help make breakfast.

I told her I was tired and she chuckled.

"You're tired?! Imagine what it's like for someone my age."

We started by cleaning a few of the plates and I wondered why they didn't do that straight after they had been used when it would have been much easier. The water was cold and properly cleaning the plates was impossible. Years of poor housekeeping meant that fossilised remains of ancient meals clung like concrete to what had once been the surface. Poppy told me not to worry about making them sparkle and I smiled to myself, knowing it would have been impossible.

We made some herbal tea and went out into the countryside to pick some fruit. As we walked, Poppy told me that they used to grow all their own food.

"Some of the newer arrivals felt that it was a little too much work and stopped them from spending time searching for answers."

When the meagre-looking breakfast had been laid out Poppy and I were still the only ones around. She told me about the group session we would have later that day.

"It's all about asking each other questions so that we can see if we're all searching for the right answer. Willow is such a wonderful guide. He can sense how to lead us all to the same point in the most effective of ways. He's very spiritual, you know?"

Eventually the others began to emerge. When more were awake than asleep, Willow called us all together. The group search session took place in the tent because it had started to rain outside. We all sat down in a circle and heard the rain tapping the canvas as Willow began.

"First, I would like us all to observe a ten-minute silence. As we have been forced into the tent by the wonderful power of nature, we will observe introflection rather than extroflection."

"Praise nature!" Everyone said in unison. I had missed it, but mumbled it a second later.

"We mustn't be tempted to go down the path of singularity, for sharing is the essence of meaning. Breathe in deeply."

Everyone did.

"Sharing is the essence of truth," he said.

"Sharing is beauty," everyone but me replied. I didn't know we were all supposed to reply with something, I had not been properly informed.

Willow took in four more long, deep breaths. Everyone in the circle did the same and we held the hand of the person next to us. He had said it would be a ten-minute silence but I'm pretty sure it went on for at least twenty. The silence was finally broken by Poppy and I could see Willow was a little annoyed that she had taken over.

"Who would like to start?" she asked.

Willow frowned and rephrased the question before anyone had a chance to reply.

"Who would like the honour of allowing us into your soul?"

Poppy rolled her eyes and Willow looked sternly at her.

Emerging from a daze, Elvo, one of the older members, was the first to speak. He moved slowly into the middle.

"Place your hands upon this saved soul," Willow demanded.

Elvo cleared his throat and lay down in the middle of the group, closing his eyes and wriggling on his back until he was comfortable.

"Tell us the answers you seek."

He breathed deeply four times.

"Is water like visible air?"

Willow nodded with approval.

"Yes, because we are all as one, just as water and air are one and one with us. What is your answer?"

"I think they are the same. But water is the air that we can see."

"Now let's question the answer," Willow said looking at Poppy. She nodded with half-closed eyes while she gathered her thoughts.

"Why does air hide from us?" she said.

Elvo tensed a little, I could feel it under my hand.

"There is something that it does not want us to know," Elvo said.

"Just as the universe hides the answer from us, air may be hiding the answer but as it is like water, we can see its secrets through rivers and lakes. What is your answer?"

"We must look to water when we question air," Elvo replied.

The group looked to Poppy to question the answer.

"We must learn about what is hidden by knowing more about what is not. What questions should we ask of water?"

It was Elvo's turn again.

"We must ask why it tells us the secrets of air."

"We have gotten closer!" Willow decreed. "To find the answer, we must now search water to tell us about air. This will tell us more about how we are all one."

Elvo's face lit up. Everyone looked to Poppy.

"We must thank our brother Elvo, for he has shown us that we can search through what is known to discover the unknown. Now we can move closer to the answer to everything we seek."

Everyone took their hands off Elvo and swayed as he took his seat back in the circle. They started chanting, "We are one, we know more, we thank you and ourselves."

"Introflection!" Willow commanded and everyone closed their eyes again. I was bewildered by all of this and hadn't the time to properly consider whether I was hearing things that were profound or utterly ludicrous. I knew that I was either surrounded by people too intelligent for me to understand or extraordinary idiocy.

"Another sibling!" Willow said, looking to the group.

Sarah, one of the younger members of the group stood up, moved into the middle of the circle and lay down. We all made sure that at least one part of us was touching her.

"Tell us the answers that you seek," Willow continued.

Sarah sighed deeply. "It's a strange one today."

Poppy closed her eyes piously.

"There is no wrong way to search, my dear. You are safe from judgement here." I felt as though Poppy was speaking on my behalf a little out of turn, but I didn't contradict her.

"Open yourself to us," Willow said. "Allow us in. It's greatness that awaits an honest search."

Sarah readied herself through an impressive routine of strange breaths and then spoke with a renewed vigour.

"I'm thinking about leaving to try and live a more modern life, to search for answers by observing nature from outside of it."

Poppy spluttered, her cheeks flaring up with patchy redness. For a few breaths she was straining to get the words out until eventually they came.

"Sarah, my dear child, you mustn't search for answers that way, they will never come. Only the lost search from the outside, and you are a found soul."

"A found soul," everyone repeated together.

"Why do you wish to wonder?" Willow asked.

"I know I'm found, but I feel lost," Sarah said, trying hard to find the right way to explain her innermost thoughts. "I've found no answers, only questions. I think I need to find out if more answers will come if I try something different, knowing that I can always come back if I'm wrong."

"The questions *are* the answers," said Willow. "All the questions lead us closer to *the* answer. You need to let the questions in. It's only through more questions that the answer can be found."

"But I am so confused by the questions. They fill my mind and I can't think clearly."

"That is perfect, my dear," Poppy replied immediately. "The path to clarity emerges from the forest of confusion."

"Let's take your questions," Willow interrupted sternly. "You are looking to go elsewhere to find clarity. But you will you only find more confusion. What is your answer?"

"That I should go elsewhere to find clarity."

"No, my child. This creates the question, how will you find clarity elsewhere?" Poppy replied.

"By seeking out different approaches."

"No," said Willow. "This is the wrong answer. The other approaches will only lead to more confusion because they do not seek the answer at all costs."

Poppy moved towards Sarah and put her hand on her forehead. "This confusion shows us how important it is that you stay."

"We shall hear no more, poor soul," Willow declared. "We need to give you time."

Sarah was not allowed to say anything else. They moved on with two more volunteers, both of whom were searching for deeper meaning through questions such as "Who am I?" and "Who should I be?"

Eventually, Willow's attention turned to me and I lay in the middle of the circle. Everyone made sure that they were touching me. I was a little anxious.

"Our new sibling will go through the genesis questioning," Willow told the group, his head bowed devoutly.

"What does your heart seek?" he continued softly.

"I want to be real," I told him instinctively, shocking myself. The circle began to sway as though I'd triggered a group reaction.

Willow placed his hand on my forehead. "Let's all do this together for our new sibling."

"Why?" The swaying circle all asked in unison.

Willow glanced over and I realised the question was directed at me.

"Because nothing matters if you're not real," I said.

"Why?" the circle enquired, louder than before.

"Because there are no consequences here."

"Why?" I was asked, the noise getting louder and now it felt a little aggressive.

"Because we are all imaginary."

"Why?" They were shouting, working themselves into a frenzy.

"There is no why. We were made this way."

"Why?" The noise was becoming deafening.

"Because real people need an imagination."

"Why?" Louder still.

"Because they need to be able to pretend."

"Why?"

I felt condemned.

"I don't know why."

"Why?" they shouted.

I wanted them to stop.

"Because I've never been told."

"Why?" It was getting too intense.

"Because nobody knows."

"Why?" They could not get louder.

"Because it's impossible to find out."

"Why?" It was becoming more chaotic.

"Because we don't know how to get the information."

"Why?" I was running out of answers.

"Because we don't know where to look for it."

"Why?"

My mind was stopping.

"Because nobody has discovered *where* to look for it."

"Why?"

I was finished.

"I don't know."

"Why?'

"I just don't."

"Why?"

I was getting frustrated, wishing they would stop and finally Willow came to my rescue.

"OK, enough."

I breathed for the first time since we had started. I was relieved but bewildered that I had become so absorbed in something I was so sceptical of only moments before.

"We have seen the answers," Willow said. "They are good but they are not complete. Now do you see how we all share the same question? All of us are one through the questions we ask."

I was given some more of the bitter drink that they had given me the night before. I took more than two sips this time. It was deeply comforting.

10.

Poppy was rubbing my back as I sat on the floor outside the sleeping tent where an array of cushions had been strewn. I hadn't asked her to do it but she seemed to be enjoying herself and it was pleasant enough.

The comforting touch made me think back to J and the peak of our young love. We would go to a hidden part of your mind, a place where we could be alone and confident that we would never be found. Even if an Arrow had searched for us, they would have seen where we were but struggled to understand how to get there. There was a supernatural element to it, a world built as a fortress for our sweetest moments where only the beloved could reside. Only Philip would ever search for us and even he would know that if we were there, he should leave us alone or risk our joint anger.

The world was within a deep oasis in the middle of a vast desert. To get to it we had to dive down where the depth of the clear water made the oasis floor impossible to see, holding our breath until we reached a giant rock that stood completely alone. The rock looked like the face of a God, as though it had once sat majestically within the halls of a great temple but had ended up lost, hidden in this obscure place for reasons long forgotten. We'd arrive at the rock with our lungs burning and swim into the mouth of the godlike structure where a cavern, lit with a gigantic glittering chandelier would welcome us with its wonderful, cool air. The cavern was lined with doors, all of which led to places that changed every time they were opened. But underneath the carpet, directly under the chandelier was a trap door that took us to a vison of another dimension. The world there was full of different colours that do not exist anywhere else. There were trees of water that hung off the ground and would change shape whenever we ran through them. The suns were less bright and warm but there were hundreds juggled over the skies. We could look at each one without hurting our eyes and gravity would shift as they moved. The ground was soft, like a fluffy bed with silk sheets and a gentle hum of music always softly played, changing with our mood.

It was our special place. It was where we experimented with tenderness and improved the ways that we had discovered of making each another tingle. The soft brushes of my hand upon J's back were replaced by gentle kisses. The goosepimples that had made us giggle before became bigger and appeared everywhere, pulling our skin taut. I would kiss J's eyes and want the taste to dissolve into me and become part of my body too. We started to allow one another to see parts of ourselves that only we had seen before. We made each other shiver with delight, allowing our instincts to take control and when we became tired, we rested in one another's arms.

Sometimes I would fall asleep and wake to the sensation of J's finger gently moving upon my lips. I'd open my eyes to a vision of perfection, regaining consciousness while J's warmth enveloped me and the delicious tingles would return again. The thought of leaving our hidden world was rarely welcomed by either of us. It became a museum of the sentimental. Even a forgotten and crumbling wall had become awash with meaning, simply because we had leant against it together, years ago.

These memories had made me temporarily forget where I was but a rustle of people moving against the tent floor brought me back to the present and the comfort of Poppy's hands rubbing my back.

"How are you settling in?" Poppy asked me, as though she believed I would be there for a long time. In truth, I wasn't sure how long I'd stay.

"I'm finding this all rather strange."

"Of course you are. It's because it's different and different things are always strange to begin with."

"But it's more than that. I don't think I understand what all of this is achieving. Do you really believe that you will ever find a single answer to explain everything?"

"Maybe *I* won't. But eventually someone else might. We all need to work together, you see?"

"But why not try a more scientific approach?"

Poppy stopped rubbing my back and allowed herself to fall slowly forward on to her elbow, lying on her side so she could see my face.

"Scientific? My child, do you believe that people really think what they think? Or do they just think that they think what they think?"

I took a little time to try and translate what Poppy had said in to some sort of meaning.

"What's the difference?"

"Whether or not we are free to think at all." Poppy said. "Science has it's uses, my child. But it understands nothing of the soul. That's what you really need to understand because everything is really just what your soul tells you."

"That's ridiculous." I said immediately.

"We must never be too judgemental about what is and isn't ridiculous, my child. Nobody is honest to the judgemental and if all you hear are lies, you will start to believe them," she said.

She smiled, her eyes darting upwards and downwards as though she were astutely aware of something about me and was confirming it to herself. I smiled back instinctively, enjoying the growing familiarity of her mannerisms. I was starting to find them calming. I felt very safe whenever she was close and even though I didn't always understand what motivated her, I sensed that underpinning everything she did was a powerful kindness.

She stood up. "Let's walk."

We meandered towards the fire pit where Sarah and Elvo were practicing a flamboyant dance move whilst the run-away king watched, cross-legged and leaning backwards on his hands. We all acknowledged one another with subtle nods. I was starting to feel a friendliness towards this strange group despite my growing bewilderment with what they were trying to achieve.

"I should go back to my normal life soon," I told Poppy as the camp fell further into the distance.

"Why don't you bring it here?"

I giggled. "I'm not too sure that anyone else I know would understand this place."

"They could give it a chance, couldn't they?"

"Yes, I suppose they could. But I know that they wouldn't"

"Why not?"

"Because they would find it bizarre."

Poppy was silent. I knew that she admired honesty and I didn't want to belittle her life's work but I was struggling to see anything of substance in the way she searched for truth.

"You have all been so welcoming to me. But I just find so much of what you do and say complete nonsense."

"Ah! I knew it."

"I enjoy the weirdness. It's fun. And I enjoy spending time with everyone. But I don't understand what you are looking for."

"I know, my child. You are different, after all. Maybe for you the answer is different too."

"What answer? I don't understand what answer you are trying to find."

"Neither do we."

"So how do you know it's worthwhile?"

"How do you know it isn't worthwhile?"

"Because it doesn't help you to understand anything useful."

"Why not?"

"Because it doesn't give you the information you need to change anything. I mean, science helps us understand everything around us. Your answers do nothing."

Poppy looked bemused.

"Your mind is very far away from where it needs to be," she said.

The path we had been walking along had started to fade away into wild grass. Slightly beyond us was a tree that stood alone in a meadow. We moved towards it and sat down under the shade of its swaying branches, looking back towards the tents we'd left behind.

"Don't you think it's interesting to consider whether water holds the secrets of air?" Poppy asked.

"Maybe it's interesting but it's just a mental journey. It doesn't mean anything. It's just nonsense."

"Why do you say that?"

"Because water and air are different. Everyone knows they're different. They don't have minds, they can't hide secrets, it's just playing with words and going on thought journeys."

"Why aren't thought journeys important?"

"Because they don't help us to do anything."

"How do you know?"

"Because they don't lead anywhere. It's all hypothetical."

"How do you know that what you are searching for is not also completely hypothetical?"

"Because reality is exactly the opposite of hypothetical."

"Or is it?"

"Stop talking in questions all the time!"

Poppy sighed deeply.

"My dear child, you can rarely be sure of anything. However, I am very sure of two things: journeys taken with the mind are always worthwhile and *you* should spend more time taking them seriously."

"Why?"

"You look at the world in the wrong way. You clearly place so much importance on science and reality but these are also journeys you are taking with your mind, my child. Science is only a search for things that we can all perceive together. You shouldn't ignore the things that only you can perceive yourself. How do you know reality is not hypothetical?"

"Because I've felt it!" I said, surprising myself. I'd never even alluded to the dream about J in front of anyone before. I paused in amazement at what I was about to say. But her lack of judgement and kindness made me feel comfortable confiding in her.

"I've felt reality," I whispered. "I've been part of something that was different. It felt different. It felt real."

"It probably was," she said.

I let out a bit of air, a half-laugh, an attempt to dismiss what had been said as ridiculous. It was an instinctive reaction but then I started to properly consider what Poppy was telling me.

I turned slightly so that I was facing her.

"What do you mean?" I asked.

Poppy smiled and I saw her eyes drifting, moving away from my face to look at all of my body, then the tree, then the landscape. "The most obvious things are often the hardest to notice. I could tell you what you probably already know but it wouldn't be as satisfying as realising it for yourself, would it?"

She leant her head back against the tree trunk and took a luxurious breath.

"Who am I to you?"

"Poppy," I said.

"Yes, of course I am. But look at me. Why do you think I am the way I am?"

I didn't know.

"Why are any of us the way we are?" I asked.

Poppy looked away as if to find another way of explaining herself.

"Why indeed? Well, all of us are not really in control of who we are. But whereas I have very little control over who you are, you have quite a lot of control over who I am."

"How?"

"My dear, stop and think for a moment. Have you ever felt as though you are a bit different to everyone else?"

"Yes, all the time!"

"Why?"

"I don't know why," I said.

"If you don't understand why, you don't understand anything."

I thought for a while and still couldn't make out where Poppy was going or whether the journey would be worthwhile.

"Why do you think you are different?" she asked.

"Surely everyone does, don't they?".

"Maybe. But why do you?"

I was getting frustrated and pushed my feet out so that they scraped and disturbed the earth.

Poppy gave me a moment longer to think but I said nothing.

"Let me put it this way, I suspected the very first moment we met that you were different. Now I know for sure that you are. How do you think that's possible?"

I screwed up my face. I had no idea what she was talking about. Poppy thought for a while and then tried again.

"Do you think I'm different or just like everyone else?"

"You're different, of course, everyone is!"

"We all think we are different. It's one thing we all have in common."

"Where is this going?"

"Look at me." Poppy covered her wrist with her hand and I held it up so I could look at it.

"Am I wearing a bracelet?" she asked.

"I can't remember."

"Yes or no?"

I shrugged my shoulders. "I don't know. Yes?"

"What does it look like? And don't say, 'I don't know.'"

"It's green. And it has yellow patterns on it." I guessed.

"What patterns?"

"Swivels. Roundish swivels."

Poppy raised her eye brows then looked down at her wrist and moved her hand. On her wrist was a green bracelet with yellow roundish swivels.

"I didn't know I had this bracelet until you told me."

And then finally I began to see. I began to understand what I had always known but never realised.

Poppy looked at me with a reassuring seriousness.

"It's OK. Nobody else knows who you are either. Only me."

Pulses of curiosity flowed through my head, making me feel dizzy. I became ravenous for knowledge. I wanted to consume it, for it to come more quickly than it could be given.

Poppy took my hand.

"Does everyone feel different because they are all different? Or is it because you feel different and it's reflected in your creations?"

Poppy started to spin her new bracelet around her wrist.

"I'm not sure I existed until I met you. Now, I know I didn't. None of us exist without you here to create us."

I felt my heart beating roughly through my body.

"That is why science will never give *you* the answer, my child. You would just be creating the science that you discover."

I had always thought that my world was like yours, that everything outside of me, every person, every object was entirely independent. But Poppy had opened my eyes to the truth. I am the only one who can give your imagination any meaning. Poppy is continually created by me, reflective perhaps of something that is part of us but we've never known before. She is impossible without me perceiving that she exists first.

I looked around us, at the trees, the grass, the other people wandering through the landscape and suddenly I realised that none of them knew you like I did. None of them look like you or think like you. None of them are you. But I am. It made me feel powerful and important. I enjoyed it and Poppy noticed.

"We live in the imagination. Nothing feels real!" Poppy told me, her face alive with happiness. "But I've heard it whispered about before, the feeling of reality within an imaginary event. It is something very different because if it feels real, it's more of an experience, after all, don't you think?"

I stopped. I breathed. Slowly I began to regain control of my thoughts. Poppy could see that I was more focused.

"The moment I first saw you, I thought you had a presence that felt strangely important, as though my life depended on you. Now I know it does! My dear child, when you feel that something is real, it must be. I've never felt that. I don't know anyone other than you who has. It must be impossible unless you are connected deeply with something real. And you are. You are the most special person here."

Poppy picked up my hand and placed it on my heart.

"You are the soul."

I doubted her. 'The soul' felt too obscure.

"You must feel it, don't you? You're different from everyone else. You're not *part* of the mind we all live within, you *are* the mind. You are the creator."

"But I'm not...I can't just create things. Everything is already created."

"Yes," Poppy replied. "But created, subconsciously, by you. It's not something you have to think about, my child, it's not even something that you may feel you can control."

"I can't control it! I didn't think about you or make you up, you just appeared in front of me."

"That's probably how it feels. You don't consciously do anything but it doesn't mean that it isn't you doing it."

We spent a moment looking into each other's eyes. Everything had become deeply serious.

"But I'm not telling you what to say," I said. "You're just saying it and telling me things that I never realised."

Poppy chuckled a little, breaking the tension. "Well, maybe that's true. Or maybe you just don't realise that you're telling me what to say. But you've created me now, as I am, so you can't uncreate me. And anyway, I'm only telling you things that I already know and I can only know them because you have allowed me know them."

"How do you know that nobody else has realised who I am?"

"Because, for some reason, you have given me that knowledge."

She paused and made sure I was paying complete attention.

"It might not feel like you are making everything up as you go along but that doesn't stop it from being true. You are part of our God, my child. You have the power of creation."

My thumping heart felt as though it were controlling me, not the other way around. I needed some time alone and walked out into the fresh wind that blew against my skin. Soon the only sound was the gentle whisper of the breeze over my ears. It made me feel alone and, in my loneliness, I could start to think clearly once more.

I felt so wholly a part of the imagination I was in. As I looked out, I started to realise that I was really looking into your mind and into ourselves. I felt a burden and then a loneliness, a sudden realisation that everyone I loved and everyone I knew was simply another part of me, of your mind, of us.

Although I had felt different my whole life, I had never dared to believe that I really was. I imagined that it was a feeling everyone shared but now I allowed myself to believe what I had always instinctively known. I am alone in your imaginary world. When you are not here, it is me, not you, creating what is around me.

As I considered this, a guilt that had been forgotten for a while returned. Nothing imaginary just happens. Either you or I imagine it first, or we do it together. We influence one another. You don't decide on your dreams, we decide them between us.

When we watched what happened to J, we weren't just bystanders. I had created the scene and then allowed the consequences to infect a world where you are not present. I realised that I wasn't just responsible for what happened in the dream, I was responsible for everything. I was responsible for creating J, for creating all the evil in the imagination itself.

I knew you wanted to leave the dream, that you were shocked by what was happening and where I had taken you. I made you watch J go through misery. Why? I couldn't answer that. I had no idea what led me to create such a hideous thought. For curiosity? How could I be so evil? The realisation that I was solely to blame for everything bad made me tremble. I decided I needed to see J again. It became an urgent desire, so I simply left, calling out for J and rushing away from Poppy and the camp.

J heard me calling and showed me where to go. Then instantly we were alone together, sitting in a field of barley. I felt wretched and then guilty for feeling so wretched because I knew everything must be so much worse for J. I tried to push all the love I had into an embrace so tight that it made me breathless. I felt J instinctively pull away from me but then slowly accept the love I was trying to convey. J was happy at such a meaningful greeting but obviously confused.

I nearly said that I knew what had happened. I nearly admitted that it was all my fault. I nearly told J that I would do whatever it took to help. But I didn't say any of those things because I knew the truth would destroy our friendship.

Instead I said, "I've missed you recently." It wasn't a lie but it felt like it was.

We sat down and said nothing for a while. "You know why I sometimes come to this spot? Do you recognise it?" J asked me.

I looked around. It seemed like any beautiful countryside setting in your imagination. I couldn't sense anything particular about it.

"This is where I became J!"

"What do you mean?"

"I can't remember anything before. We were right here, where we are sitting now. You were with Alice and Philip and I started becoming who I was out of nothing. I saw you look at me and it was as though I had always been here, part of the group and immediately I knew that you loved me."

"By the way I looked at you?"

"Yes. I thought that if a look could make me feel so warm, it must be because it was full of love. It was the first feeling I ever had, the feeling of being loved by you. I loved you back immediately and it was easy even though I didn't understand it."

I felt a weight in my throat as I lingered on J's beautiful words and the memory, which came back to me so perfectly preserved that I could still feel the echoing rapture of that day. I lost myself for a moment in the yearning I felt to relive all those emotions that become diluted with age.

"I still love you." I said.

I felt J's hand on my thigh and a gentle squeeze.

"I know you do. I love you too. But it's different now, isn't it? You love me because of our past, not because of our future. It's still powerful but it's different from the way it was before."

J's eyes searched mine. I felt the happiness of the memory of our first day together drain away and a seriousness replace it.

"It's just as strong."

J sighed softly. "I know, of course it is. It's not stronger, or weaker, just new and different. It's the same for me. But it's not the same as when I began. Sometimes I come here just to remember it all and how it felt."

J looked towards the horizon and I gazed over the forgotten fields that had suddenly turned sacred to me, because of the emotions they spurned in J. The sun set behind the hills of the unspoilt valley and I enjoyed the feeling of sitting next to my old friend. The comfort loosened the grip of my new loneliness but did nothing to repress the relentless guilt for what I had done to J and the evil I had brought into the world.

Any happiness wasn't allowed to exist on its own, it was permanently diluted by the overwhelming knowledge that I had great power but no control. I was terrified about the future, the mistakes I would make, the destruction and corruption that I would be responsible for unless I could learn to change. I felt a need to be protective and kind, to atone for what I had done and what I might do.

I looked over at J, the embodiment of my lost innocence and I cursed myself for the place I had created. The way in which the excitement and happiness of new love fades away so easily over time. The way that things can never be unimagined. The way that I had spoilt such perfection with such brutality. The way I couldn't go on loving J as I had all those years ago and the way that, as the passion receded, I filled the gap with pity dressed as love.

It was dusk but neither of us moved.

"We can't dwell on the past for too long," J said. "Even if it's nice sometimes, it probably isn't good for us."

"I know." I moved closer so that I could place my forehead on J's.

"I love you," I said and we drifted away from one another again.

11.

At the camp, Poppy made me a warm drink using fresh leaves picked from the wild only seconds before. It was delicious.

"Why are you here, Poppy?"

"I don't know. You would know better than me."

"But I don't. I don't feel like I have any control over anything at all. I don't understand why you are spending your time doing something that seems so pointless if this is all my creation."

"I don't think it's pointless, my child."

"But *I* think that it's pointless. I mean, it's enjoyable but the questions you all ask one another, the mantras, they all seem so meaningless. And if I think that, why would I have put you here?"

"That's a brilliant question my dear. Let's think about it."

Poppy held her tea with both hands, her bracelet dangling from her wrist.

"Maybe," she began, "Maybe, it's because you needed the contrast. Maybe, if you find it all so pointless, it is so the elements of truth stand out that much more clearly."

I wasn't convinced. I frowned and Poppy attempted another explanation.

"Perhaps this is your way of telling yourself that none of this really is that pointless. Maybe it's all very important but you knew that you wouldn't be able to recognise that it was. Maybe the very fact that I find it important is to persuade you that you should find it important too."

I took a moment to think about what Poppy was saying. I was still so new to the strangeness of the knowledge Poppy had given me. Something was stopping me fully believing that Poppy was just a creation of mine, full of thoughts and feelings that I had given her but which I had no memory or knowledge of at all.

"How do you know that I am who you think I am?"

"Because you've given me that knowledge, my child."

"But what if you're wrong?"

"Do you think I am?"

"No. I instinctively thought you were right but I have no idea why. The more I've thought about it, the more I'm terrified of what it means. Or that we could both be completely wrong."

"What about my bracelet? We both watched you create it from nothing."

"How do I know you didn't always have it and that it was just a lucky guess?"

"I know it wasn't just a lucky guess. You are godly, my child."

I felt the fear return. The word, the sound of it, "godly." It made me feel so immediately proud and then desperately uncomfortable.

"But if it's true," I started until the consequences terrified me and forced me to stop again. I looked out at Poppy and saw her so clearly, her messy, mousy hair and wind-blown skin. I could smell the scent of her wild clothes and hear them rustle as she moved. She was so vividly there and outside of myself.

"If it's true, then it means I am responsible for everything. All the evil, all the horror that I've seen and sadness that people feel."

"You are only responsible for what you can control, my child. The power to create is different from the power to control. Parents can create a beautiful child but can't control the way it kicks in the womb or cries at night."

"But then what power do I have?"

"Immense power. You may not feel as though you can control what is created but that doesn't mean that you can't learn. It is perfectly normal to be blind to those things that are most important. Gods wouldn't necessarily know they were Gods if they have never been anything else. We live within the very fabric of the universe but have no idea what it is. Change shines out to all of us and captures our attention, whilst the hardest things to see are those that have always been."

I tried to think of something that had never changed. I listened and smelt, looked and thought but nothing would come to me. I felt frustrated and hopelessly lonely. I saw Poppy place her tea on the floor and noticed for the first time how small and unkempt her hands were. There were patches of old pink paint still stuck to some of her finger nails and her skin was hardened by all the work she did to keep everyone at the camp happy. Nobody helped her as far as I had noticed. All of the mundane things like preparing food, giving structure to the day and collecting firewood was done by her and her alone. She was an extraordinary person in a bizarre place that did her no justice at all. I wondered why I had created a place like this and a person like her. Or if I really had that power at all.

"I'll help you, my child," she said and I looked back up at her gentle face and the wrinkles around her eyes. I wanted her help but I couldn't see myself staying at the camp. I had grown fond of the place. It had become quite comforting and simple. There was no need to argue or worry. The biggest problem was rain when we were in the mood for sun. There were no secrets; there was no modesty; everything belonged to everyone and as soon as you lost your sense of perspective, it was a pleasant place to be. But my new perspective clung to me. Eventually I knew that I would want to explore more deeply the world that I was responsible for creating.

I looked toward the horizon and tried to make it further away, experimenting with what I could and couldn't change when I felt C and J wanting to be with me. The thought of being with them made me happy and then suddenly they were there in front of me, standing next to one another.

I loved seeing them together and I admired the way they appeared. I saw immediately the small similarities between them in the way they moved towards me, the sway in their step and glints in their eyes. It was delightful.

"Hello," they both said together.

"Who are these wonderful young people?" asked Poppy.

I introduced everyone.

"Come, my dears! Let's get to know one another."

We sat down and spoke for a while. J and C seemed to be in a good mood, too good and I couldn't understand why. It seemed mischievous. I asked them why they'd come and C answered with a forced accent, speaking playfully and around the subject.

"Ya' know. Droppin' in to say hi and stuff."

C started speaking to Poppy and asked her how long she had been here.

"Ever since I was your age, I'd imagine. I could never do anything else. I know it seems strange to those who aren't open-minded, but you can ask anyone. This is a happy place."

C smirked and looked at J. "It feels a very *hippy* place."

"Hilarious," I said to C. "Sorry, Poppy. My friends can be very judgemental."

J and C both smiled at me, knowing they had been impish but both finding it humorous that I was in the sort of place they'd found me.

"What do you do here all day?" Asked C.

Poppy lit up. "We explore each other's minds whilst searching for the foundation of truth."

"Have you found the foundation of truth?" Asked J.

"My dear, it is the search that carries the individual meaning. The foundation may never be found."

C frowned. "What does that mean?"

"Well, have you ever wondered about the purpose of your life?"

"Of course," said C.

Poppy smiled softly. "Well, my dear, so has everyone else. And finding that purpose is our collective purpose."

J looked at me inquisitively. "I doubt you've changed your purpose, have you? You've been obsessed with becoming real since I can remember."

"No. But I have to say, thanks to Poppy, I understand much more about reality."

I felt a little protective of Poppy. Despite sharing C and J's obvious scepticism about the camp itself, I wanted them to see Poppy as I did, a gem of insight within the surrounding craziness.

"So, what have you learnt?" Asked J.

I paused and Poppy immediately noticed. I felt an instinctive fear of other people knowing what I had only recently realised about myself. Poppy picked up on it immediately.

"If I may speak for you, my dear? I believe that you have realised that very little is what it seems." Poppy looked at me reassuringly then spoke to J. "You may also come to the same conclusions. For example, why do you think you exist?"

J started a little awkwardly back at Poppy and then C. "Because I am here now. And so are all of you. And we are talking."

Poppy nodded. "But we all know we're not real, don't we?"

"Yes," J said.

"So, if you are not real, do you really exist?"

"Yes, of course I exist. I'm just not real. There's a huge difference."

"And what is that?"

"Well, real things exist in the real world. Imaginary things exist in the imagination. But we all exist."

"How do you know we are in the imagination?"

C and J glanced at one another and then back at Poppy.

"How do you know we aren't?" said J.

"I don't know the answer, my dear. I'm merely pointing out that it is very difficult to know anything and what we try to do here is to know *something* by questioning *everything*."

There was a short silence while we all digested what Poppy had said. I could sense that J and C were processing Poppy's words and trying to decipher whether they were insightful or ludicrous, a cycle I had become very familiar with.

"Have you heard about the Stein experiments?" C asked.

"No, dear. What are they?"

"They are what I came to tell you about." C said, looking at me. "They're changing the world. They want volunteers."

"What exactly are these experiments?"

J looked at C and then spoke first.

"Apparently, they are able to make people experience reality."

"But more than that. They are making people able to touch the real world outside of the imagination," C added.

"Seriously?" I asked.

"Yes!" They replied in unison.

"How?"

"Nobody knows. It's top secret."

J caught my eye.

"We both want to volunteer. Seeing as becoming real is all you talk about these days, we thought we'd all go together."

Poppy changed slightly when she heard why they had come. She didn't want me to leave but could tell I was immediately intrigued.

"But you've only just settled in here, my dear. You need to give this a fair chance before you start looking to do other things."

I immediately knew that I wanted to go. It was instinctive. But I also realised that leaving may not be easy. No doubt, I would have to endure a tedious discussion with Willow and Poppy, as Sarah had done, where the appeal of this new experiment would be analysed poorly and I would be told that I was making a rash and foolish decision by becoming part of it. They'd phrase it in some ludicrous way, probably something about searching for the wrong answer and getting individualistic questions.

I couldn't immerse myself in what they were doing. I didn't believe it would lead me to truth or meaning. They were all doomed to be asking questions forever without getting to an answer. Despite this, I had learnt so much from the experience of being with them. Along with what Poppy had made me realise, I'd grown and come to understand that I was not alone, that for everyone, the most basic search for meaning was always the same. In my world it's more obvious: "How can I be more real?" But the same question exists in your world, too. Perhaps for you it's: "How can I be more than I am?" In essence they are identical questions, the same ones that echoed in my every thought, shared by everyone, everywhere, in every world.

Poppy had filled me with confidence about who I was and what my abilities were, but I knew she could not provide me with a way to use them. Since then, I had desperately hoped that I would see something in Willow and the rest of these bunch of fun renegades that I had missed before. But I still couldn't see it.

Everyone there seemed to be so desperate for a greater truth but rather than challenging themselves to find it, they became distracted with a world of endless mantras, with absurdity, with hedonism, and their unwavering belief in what they were doing. I could see how it would be comforting. Rather than doing something that may force them to confront harsh and deflating realities, they distracted themselves and believed this distraction was progress. It made them happier, and who would turn their back on happiness?

But I wanted more. I knew that this was not the way for me, it was merely another path that I could ignore without regret. It may have been one that I would have explored for longer if this chance had not come along but for my whole life I had felt completely lost because there had been nothing to help me push forward my ambition to get closer to the real world and you, my creator. These experiments felt like the biggest opportunity I had ever been given. I was ready to try something new and exciting, to launch myself into the wider world of the mind that we share.

"Why don't you come too?" I asked Poppy.

"I can't leave here!"

"You always speak about open-mindedness when you want people to see things from your perspective. Why don't you open *your* mind to new things?"

I tried to force her to say yes. I thought only of the word and as if to spite me, to show me how little control I had of my own abilities, she said;

"No."

But I remember thinking, *she'll come, it doesn't matter what she says.* And even though she had said no, we all for some reason knew that she meant the opposite and accepted it, as if it were perfectly normal.

12.

The contrast between the camp's welcoming fields and the cold hard bricks of the institution that housed Stein's experiment made Poppy strangely introverted. As we entered, she quickly grabbed my arm, as if there were pressing dangers all around us.

A similar building doesn't exist in reality, everything about it seemed to represent conflicting things. As though a beautiful stately home had been renovated into a grotesque, industrial factory. There were elements of hopelessness in its prosperity and homeliness in its misery. It seemed to demand impeccable standards of all those that entered, making it uncomfortable, oppressive but hardening, as if the building were challenging you with a snobbish certainty that you would fail. It made me want to prove the building wrong. Within its paradoxical form was the temptation of unknown delights and prestige awaiting anyone who could conquer its challenges.

We were ushered towards a hall where we joined about fifty others. All of us were rotated through a series of interviews which delved into our motivations for being there. They were happy for us to stay as a group and, for reasons that none of us understood, some people were told that they were unsuitable, while others were asked to return.

After the second interview, C was told, "Unfortunately you will not be participating in the process any longer."

C looked taken aback, obviously confused by the unexplained dismissal. It felt unjust, especially because C was the one who had found out about the experiments.

As the day moved on, I met Professor Deborah Stein for the first time. She tried to be polite but was too robotic to appear genuine. She was clearly behaving unnaturally and it gave us a very inaccurate first impression.

"Hello, thank you for coming. Good to have you here. Well done for getting this far. Good to have you here. Yes."

She looked through some notes that she'd made over the course of the day and asked Poppy if she had been in a "cult" her entire adult life.

"Yes, although we would never call it a cult. We refer to it as a commune," Poppy replied.

Stein thought this was petty but tried to hide her reaction behind an unnatural grin. We all picked up on it. Stein asked me if I had been to the "commune."

"Yes, that's where we've all come from."

"Why were you there?"

"I thought it might open my mind. I want to explore the limits of possibility. I want to become real."

"Do you think that's possible?" asked Stein. Her tone was direct, all false politeness fading quickly. Her stern eyes looked directly into mine from a gaunt and pointy face.

"Yes, of course."

"How?"

"I'm not sure. I'm searching for the answer and that's why I've come here. Isn't that what your experiments are all about?"

"Yes, indeed. But they are difficult. How much are you willing to give to explore the 'limits of possibility?'"

"Everything."

Stein seemed happy with my response.

"And you?" Stein asked J. "Why did you decide to interview for these experiments?"

"Doesn't everyone want to see if they can become real?" J replied.

"Most people. But then most people don't realise how much it takes to break down the natural boundaries of the imagination. Often the scale of the sacrifice makes them abandon what they thought they wanted. What I need to know from you is if you are willing to totally commit to what we are doing?"

"Yes, of course, that's why we're here." J replied.

"Yes, but it is it why *you* are here?"

"Yes. That's what I meant, it's why *I* am here."

Stein smiled. It was a crooked, unnatural smile. Then she got up and left.

During that first, brief interaction Stein gave very little away about herself other than her obvious ineptitude for social niceties. Afterwards we waited on uncomfortable seats in one of the many corridors of the building until we were all informed that we should come back for a second round of interviews that would be scheduled in a few days. J and I were elated. Poppy couldn't wait to leave.

"Let's go now, my dears, please. I really, really need to leave. Now."

She was breathing heavily as she spoke, looking earnestly at both of us with mild panic in her eyes. We stopped smiling and allowed ourselves to be whisked away back to the fields, where the sun was setting and the fire was being lit.

As we arrived, I noticed how differently it all appeared to me. This time the camp felt like an old school, familiar, a remnant of my past but somewhere I knew I'd never spend much time in the future. I sat around the fire for what would probably be the last time while nostalgia arrived ahead of itself.

Poppy looked at me as we sat down on the dirty rugs near the fire.

"Don't go," she whispered. "I don't trust anything about Stein. I have a sense about people, you know I do. There is something deeply evil about her."

I knew. I sensed it too but it didn't matter. I believed the evil would achieve more than Poppy's kindness and I wanted to feel as though I was moving forward to greater truths, to the limits of possibility, towards becoming real.

Every one of us within your imagination thinks becoming real is impossible and yet it remains a deep, almost universally shared aspiration. Poppy had given me a valuable gift, a deeper knowledge of who I was and where I existed. But she couldn't tell me what to do with that information. When she tried to stop me from leaving, she hadn't spoken with any conviction, just desperation. But it was a desperation born from kindness, from caring, and from her deeply held belief in what she was doing which constrained her like a prison. I didn't think that Poppy or life at the camp could teach me anything more.

J was next to me, desperately uncomfortable in the commune, a place that had lost its appeal for me as well. I knew my time would be better spent somewhere else that evening, away from the madness. J was clearly nervous about what we had decided to become involved with. All our earlier excitement had been consumed by a lingering fear of the unknown. J needed my support. I felt the same. I didn't want to go through this alone and I wanted J by my side. We needed to leave, to be alone and to give one another confidence.

I told Poppy I was leaving and begged her to be happy for me. She looked at the floor, dodging my eyes, her old, motherly and kind body shrinking in on itself.

"You can be happy here. You can be happy *here!*"

I knew I couldn't. I told Poppy I loved her. It wasn't a lie, but it wasn't exactly true either. I felt something. It felt similar to love but not as strong. It was a deep concern, a gratefulness. Something that was generous but not all-consuming. As I stood up to leave, I felt immediately as though I was losing something. It was my fault, I was throwing it away, but I knew I would still feel its loss. Poppy would soon be out of sight and I suspected, although I wouldn't admit it to myself, that she would stay that way forever.

Poppy started to cry. There was silence before she breathed deeply. She finally looked at me and I could see her tears on her round cheeks. She spoke softly so that J could not hear.

"Stein terrifies me. She'll soon realise who you are and then she'll never let you go. She only cares about herself."

Something unspoken made me understand that Poppy wasn't telling me this to keep me with her any longer. It was a final warning.

13.

I wonder, even now, how much I changed after Poppy told me who I was. I felt stronger, proud even. For the first time I had confidence that I was capable of something, a reason to feel special. With Stein, I was being given the opportunity to be part of an experiment that claimed to be "world changing." I felt good. I had direction. I had glorious friends and the future felt exciting.

As J and I spent a few days with the others before we returned to Stein, I stopped thinking about Poppy and enjoyed my new sense of purpose. But Philip, for a reason none of us understood, seemed concerned.

"I can't put my finger on it. There just feels as though there is something not quite right. How much do you know about what you are getting yourselves into?"

"Nothing really," J said. "But we haven't started yet, we are still being interviewed."

"I know, but what for?"

"I think we'll know more about that when they've chosen us. What do we have to lose? If it's all a load of nonsense, we'll just leave."

Alice was generally ambivalent but supportive.

"You young things! Adventure, adventure, adventure. You wouldn't catch me volunteering so wholeheartedly for something that sounds so utterly incoherent."

"You would say that. You've lost your taste for life!" C teased her.

"Well, perhaps. Anyway, good luck to you. Just make sure you don't get absorbed in something before you know anything about it."

"Is there *anything* you know about it?" asked Philip.

"Well, we know it's changing the world," said C.

J and I stayed silent, intensely aware that both of us knew very little but allowing ourselves to be reassured by C's confidence.

"How is it changing the world?" Philip continued. "Surely if that were true then we all would have heard about it."

"You have heard about it!" said C with a cheeky grin.

"I mean from somewhere else. How did you hear about it?"

C sighed. "I just knew about it. Everyone's talking about it. As soon as I heard I told all of you. I don't know why you're so worried, it makes sense that the details need to be secret."

"I'm just not sure whether you should be getting involved in something you know nothing about," Philip said, scowling at me and J. "I mean, it all seems fascinating but from what you've said about the questions you were asked, it's not as if this is something trivial."

"I wish you would give them a break. It's hardly a risk to try something new, is it?" said C, ruffling Philip's hair in a way that would have annoyed him.

Philip was an enigma. He seemed to be in favour of the experiments but hated the idea of anyone he knew becoming involved. We put this down to him wanting to protect us; he saw himself as an older brother and always had. But I wonder, knowing what I know now whether there was more to it than that.

As an Arrow, Philip was able to see and sense more than we could. This meant that he had experienced more. Arrows have a duty to stop the world of your imagination becoming damaged. It is easy for things to hide within the mind and only Arrows are able to find anything, wherever it is. So those things that destroy the mind can only be found and dealt with by Arrows. We jokingly refer to them as "imagination police." It's largely an affectionate term because, while they do police the imagination, they do it so that it stays healthy. They are revered in the same way as ancient kings and queens would have been. Philip was one of the most powerful Arrows to have existed, so, when Philip told us he was concerned, we listened.

"You're making me nervous, Philip. I think you should stop being miserable; I was excited until you started talking," J told him.

J's words had the right impact. Philip became a little more light-hearted and despite the anxious excitement that accompanied J and I, we enjoyed ourselves until it was time to return to Stein. We said our goodbyes and, as we left, I looked back one last time to see C waving. I found myself unable to look away, as though I were staring at a beautiful dream.

I could sense something changing. The problem with fantasies is they're always somewhat unobtainable, otherwise they wouldn't be fantasies. C was electric and perfect but never possible. Now I had started to feel another level of happiness when we were together and it was being obviously reciprocated. Even our goodbye embrace was held longer and seemed to have more meaning within it. C, a fantasy, seemed to be becoming ever more possible, and I didn't know why.

The changes I'd noticed in C were all I could think about until J and I entered the colossal entrance hall of Stein's institution, where a man with a clipboard pointed to seats and told us to wait. The hall echoed with whispered conversations and the loud clicks of heavy soled shoes landing on the stone floor. It was incredibly impersonal and intimidating. The chairs were wooden and uncomfortable but we were made to sit on them for hours and given no information at all. It was a huge relief when we heard our names called by someone in white clothes who had appeared in front of us hours after we had arrived.

He led us up an oak staircase to a series of intersecting corridors, each one hosting hundreds of doors. Every so often, we would pass by a thick window that allowed us to look into a room as we passed. We glanced nosily through them and saw all sorts of experiments being conducted. Some on people, some on large pieces of equipment. Other rooms seemed to be completely empty and sterile. Eventually we arrived at a door that was larger than the others. The man knocked on it and it was opened from inside by a woman in another crisp white outfit. Beyond her, Stein appeared, sitting behind a large varnished desk, looking at documents rather than us. We were ushered in and told to sit on two green leather chairs opposite her.

"Thank you for coming." She said.

When J and I saw Stein again it was very clear to me that she was going to have a huge impact on my life. The strength of her character meant that every word she spoke became part of the atmosphere and had to be taken seriously.

"What we are doing here is probably the most important thing that is happening outside of the real world."

It felt like minutes before she said anything else. Her confidence was overwhelming. She felt no awkwardness in holding long silences, as there seemed to be no doubt in her mind that each one of them would be kept until she decided to speak again.

Her name was Professor Deborah Stein but we always called her Stein. For some reason she wanted it that way and it seemed in keeping with her direct manner and the impersonal nature of the institution. Everyone seemed to follow her rather than work with her. She was extraordinarily powerful and behind her trailed a cape of ferocity that fluttered fear and obedience into these followers. She was not kind like Poppy; she didn't pretend to be.

Stein ignored us for another couple of minutes and the room cleared. Eventually she passed both J and me a piece of paper. On it were a number of clauses that made us agree that we were willingly participating in "testing" and would not appeal to Arrows under any circumstances. I had never seen anything like it before and I knew Philip would be furious if he ever found out that we'd signed it. But we did, it was the only way to move forward and we were quivering with excitement. I felt as though I was looking up at a mountain peak, full of energy and self-belief, knowing I would get to the top. But this document also signalled to me that we were becoming involved in something outside of the normal laws of the mind, something consequential and potentially very savage indeed.

Stein took back the signed pieces of paper, tapping their edges on the desk so that they were perfectly aligned before neatly putting them down. She looked at each of us a couple of times.

"Why are you here?" she said.

J and I glanced at one another but said nothing.

"One of you, come on."

"Like we said last time, we want to be real." J replied.

Stein sighed impatiently and arched her head backwards slightly.

"Time for a little more detail," she said.

J told her it was because the experiments were breaking new ground but Stein immediately interrupted.

"That's what everyone says," she said. "Why do *you* personally want to do this?"

J tried to think on the spot and mumbled something about knowing we were closer to reality than we thought.

I froze because I had anticipated what the next question would be.

"How do you *know* that?"

J stopped and immediately blushed. I realised for the first time exactly why J felt touching reality was possible. I'd never considered it before that moment, but it suddenly became so clear to me. The J I saw in front of me, the J who was answering these difficult questions, was the same J that had been damaged by the dream. It was the same J that had sensed the same genuine horror and guilt that you had felt about it. The real emotions attached to that dream, the ones you have long forgotten now, meant J sensed a closeness to the real world in the same way I had.

J was in an impossible situation: either talk about the rape in front of me, something that had never been discussed before, or hide it and make something up.

"Come on!" Stein pushed. "The experiments we're doing are going to be significantly harder than answering a few questions."

J's face was flushed but determined.

"I had a horrible experience once. It was a while ago now. It was different from anything else that has ever happened to me. There was something real about it, I know there was. It ruined my life."

Stein pounced immediately, demanding to know more. I couldn't cope watching J becoming more agitated and desperately trying to avoid reliving the disgusting experience that had profoundly impacted both of our lives. So, I interrupted with something irrelevant about how I believed becoming more than you are is the most important thing to strive for. I was simply making noise, it was senseless.

Stein told me to be quiet.

She pointed her pen at J.

"You. What is it that happened to you that was so awful it has had consequences?"

J looked at me and said, "I don't want to tell you."

Stein let out a sigh and looked at us condescendingly.

"You were abused, weren't you? But it didn't feel imaginary. Why else would you be embarrassed?"

I couldn't look at J but I could feel a steady build-up of anger and embarrassment next to me.

"These things are not commonplace. You realise that, don't you? There is nothing real about anything we are doing. If your abuse felt real and still hurts you now, it's because it was an experience, not a thought."

J was close to tears and I had no idea what to do. I tried to provide some comfort by offering one of my hands but it was clear that J was reliving parts of the experience and no meaningless gesture could provide a distraction.

J turned to me. "It was in the old hall when we were younger. Just before we were supposed to meeting one another."

I wanted to say that I knew. I wanted to be truthful. It was the perfect time to be truthful but I couldn't do it. My own cowardice blocked all my good intentions. How could I have let J suffer in silence for so many years? I felt so much guilt, so much self-hatred.

"I should have told you but I felt so ashamed," J said.

I was shaking. I told J that there was nothing to feel ashamed about. I put too much emphasis on the words and began to feel terrified that I might be exposed as the one who created the horror in the first place.

I got up and wrapped J in my arms. For the first time since that horrible day, J didn't shudder at the contact and we rocked back and forth for a few moments in what would have been such a genuine snapshot of friendship if my mind hadn't been so concentrated on my guilt rather than J's feelings. I meant that embrace and I never wanted it to end. It felt like the most important contact I had ever had. I wanted it to pass over all the undelivered kindness that had been trapped within me for years. I wanted J to feel how much love and friendship I was willing to give, to know that there would never be any need to feel alone.

But it was just an embrace. It couldn't change the past and all the essential sentiments remained unspoken.

Stein, clearly finding this tedious, told us that it was important to press on. She looked down at her notes as if to give me a moment to return to my seat.

"Who was there?" Stein asked J.

"Just the man. Nobody else."

"Who was he?"

"I don't know. I've never seen him before or since."

"You must know." Stein glared at J. "It's important," she continued. "If we know who is part of an experience it will significantly help us. Try to remember."

J paused, clearly trying to remember the tormentor.

I kept quiet, thinking back to that day. I had never seen the man before either, he was just a character made up by us within the dream. He could never be found again and it wouldn't matter because he was unimportant. Stein wasn't really searching for him. She was searching for the person that created the dream, the one that created her, the one that was sitting opposite her right now. I knew how important my secret was and I instinctively wanted to hide it because I didn't want J to hate me.

"I don't know. I can't remember," J said.

"Which is it?"

"Both."

Stein sighed unsympathetically and moved on. "And you?" she said, looking at me. "Why are you here?"

It took me longer to reply than it would normally. To have something so sobering lingering within the room meant I had to try to grasp control back from my wandering mind before I could talk.

I spoke for a while about how much I wanted to know whether it was possible to become more real. Every time I finished speaking, Stein asked me, "Why?" until finally I said, "Because why would you know that it's possible and not want to become real?"

Stein immediately asked me how I knew it was possible.

I was treading carefully and I knew Stein was probing for the sort of sincerity I was not willing to give.

"Because I believe so much that it is possible, it has become possible within my mind."

Stein laughed at me.

"That's idiotic." She wrote something down in her notes. "But not necessarily unhelpful."

She went to a cupboard and brought out a small bottle.

"This is a poison. It hurts."

She took a small amount of the green liquid into a syringe and told me to hold out my hand. She allowed a single drop to fall onto my palm. Nothing happened at first. It felt like warm water. She watched me and I watched my palm.

Then my hand started to get a little red and a warmth pulsed in my palm. Then a numbness came and my hand began to throb as though it were swelling. But I was looking at it and it was fine, just a little red.

Stein told me that it would start to hurt soon and that I would need to channel my enthusiasm to be real into dealing with the pain. I could see J was nervous on my behalf.

The pain started to intensify and soon it felt as though I had been stung and the venom was spreading from my hand. Then it was as if the room had turned into an expanding foam that stole all the air. In the thud of a heartbeat, I felt suffocated and became immersed in a pain so intense it was as if nothing else could exist. I think I started to scream, then I collapsed and rolled on the floor. Everything went black. I bit my wrist to try to distract myself with a more familiar pain but Stein calmly told me to stop before I did more permanent damage.

I writhed around in concentrated misery until I had no energy to continue doing anything but clutch my hand and whimper, begging the pain to leave me.

Stein moved over to where I had collapsed. Her piercing eyes searched mine.

"If you can't accept the pain, this is a waste of time."

I tried to think of anything except the pain but it was too consuming. I stopped trying to breathe. J ran over and held my head, telling me that everything would be alright.

On it went. I believed I was going to die. I remember preparing myself to embrace death and I was happy because it would save me from the pain. But then my thoughts changed and I was in the room again. The pain started to fade and with every pulse it became more manageable. It was stopping, slowly shrinking before it completely disappeared and I started to love the feeling of simple normality. I felt no anger.

J was traumatised and couldn't speak.

Stein began to leave the room. "If you come back in a week, I'll know you're serious."

14.

That night we went to Alice's house. Tucked deep within the hills, we were all together once again. I was explaining what had happened, avoiding saying anything that may have embarrassed J, but growing ever more frustrated as I heard myself speak. I spoke of my agony and portrayed a scene of torture. I spoke of Stein's words and portrayed a mad woman. I could understand how retelling what Stein had done would lead people to believe that I was some sort of victim but I didn't feel that way about it at all. No matter how hard I tried, I couldn't properly describe that despite what had happened, I believed that Stein's experiments were the best possible thing I could be doing.

Alice was bewildered. "Why on earth would you go back now? The woman is insane!"

Philip was livid and shouted at us as if he owned our lives and that by the force of his will alone could change the future.

"It's barbaric! What on earth gives her the right to do that to you without any warning whatsoever? There's no way you're going back now."

"Surely the whole point is that they didn't know what was coming?" C was our only defender. "If they knew what was coming, it wouldn't have been a genuine test."

"Test? A test of what? How stupid people can be? How much you can hurt someone and still get them to come back?" Philip roared.

"No, clearly it's a test of how committed they are to the project. Why would you do something so important without knowing you are doing it with people who are committed? And anyway, it's their decision whether they want to go back, not yours. Nothing great is ever achieved without bravery, we should be here supporting them."

C was impossibly good-looking, I found it completely disarming. I often became transfixed and it spurred within me more than mere desire. You know this, of course, because C is your fantasy. Between us, we have created something so close to perfection. Sometimes looking at C stops me from being myself. If C had dismissed going back in the same way as Philip, I know it would have made far more of a difference to my decision. I might not have gone back at all.

Philip continued with his fury, making many good points along the way. I listened dutifully. The main cause of his anger was the waiver we'd signed that stripped us of protection from the Arrows. He was pacing around Alice's kitchen, his hands on his head.

"Why would you do that? Why?"

"We had to. If we hadn't, we wouldn't have been able to continue." J told him.

"It proves she is doing something that she shouldn't!"

Alice was clearly concerned by the methods that were going to be used as the tests continued.

"You are effectively volunteering for torture," she told us, looking very seriously towards the floor, her lips pursed.

There was no argument against most of what they were saying. What we were doing was not rational; it was based on a belief that the impossible was possible, something we only believed because of an experience we could not share.

I was actually impressed by the test Stein put me through. I'd thought for a while that pain might be the best way to experience something real. When you are using your imagination, you can decide to do anything you want, exactly as you want to do it and I depict it all for you. It's instinctive and I do it immediately because I know that you need me to do it. But what if I couldn't? What if I was in too much pain to consider anything else? Then you wouldn't be able to access your own imagination. Your mind would begin failing and automatically other parts of you would come to my assistance. Your body's defences would realise that some of your basic functionality was hurt and it would start searching for what it was. It would try to fix me and as it did, I would be in contact with a part of your physical body. That's where I thought there may exist an opportunity to straddle your world and mine. As far as I knew, nobody had tried this before.

I believed Stein knew what she was doing. I was determined and I could see J was too. Once you have that sort of determination and blind belief, logic doesn't change your mind. Nothing else matters anymore. I wanted to try to explore the limits of my capabilities and get as close to reality as possible.

I felt as if I had already started on a journey from which I would never return. I had found my calling. I wanted to prove that I was capable of being something greater, that I was special, that the reality I'd felt in the dream was not false. Even more than all of that, I wanted to get closer to you. I wanted you to know me, I wanted to be with you, experiencing reality beside you, rather than hidden in the world of the unreal.

I knew I was going back. And I knew J wanted to go back with me.

C was the only one who was genuinely supportive and this blessing delighted me. It was more than support. C told us that we deserved nothing but admiration, comparing us to the greatest explorers. I can't tell you how much that helped. It's pathetic, isn't it? That the tiniest bit of encouragement from people we adore can make our determination so resolute.

After a week, a turbulent week where Alice and Philip continually showed their dismay at what we were doing, J and I set off together back to Stein. We paused as we arrived to look at the gigantic and imposing building that held our future within its walls. We were excited. Stein was excited. She couldn't hide it; the emotion was obvious on her otherwise drab face. She was different this time. Just as unapproachable but more engaged. She closed the door and then sat down behind her desk.

"I'm going to ask you to do things to one another today that you won't like. You two are close, aren't you?"

J and I knew that we were but it felt strange to say so. We were silent, so Stein continued.

"J, *you* have already felt the impact the real world can have. You're one of very few that has, so you should feel a small familiarity with what it feels like to come in to contact with reality."

Stein then looked at me. "You don't have any idea what it feels like, apparently."

Stein placed her hands in front of her on the varnished surface of the large, oak desk. Her palms were down and she slid them outwards so that her presence became wider and more imposing. She started articulating every word with unnerving meticulousness.

"It is important that both of you become familiar with the feeling of reality. Very few people can deal with the pain it takes."

She paused and I nodded to show her that I understood.

Stein opened her notebook. She told us more about the experiments they were conducting, how they were not limited just to pain but that they were testing the impact of love, lust or any all-encompassing emotion that could bring us into contact with a part of the body that was physically real.

She picked up the notebook with both hands and snapped the spine so that the fresh, clear pages that had been energetically turning themselves over instead collapsed and rested, lifeless, where Stein wanted them to be.

"I am going to ask you to hurt one another."

Stein stood up and pulled back the top left drawer of the bulky desk, taking out two cylindrical metal objects. She handed one to me and one to J. Then she wrapped thick black tape around our hands so that we couldn't let the objects go. Next, she gave each of us another grip with a red button on top.

"With these buttons, you will electrocute each other," she said.

We were told this as though it were the most normal thing in the world. If you had heard her speak through a wall and couldn't decipher the words but only the tone, you'd have thought we were being asked to sit down or write our names on a piece of paper. It took a moment longer than normal to understand the meaning behind the words and exactly what was about to happen. I began to sweat and I could see that J was breathing heavily.

Stein looked authoritatively at J. "Press yours first."

J paused and looked at me, eyes open wider than normal, partly asking for my approval but also displaying a reluctance to hurt me and a shock at the position we had found ourselves in.

"Come on, quickly," Stein said. I became tense, waiting for the pain, wondering how badly the electricity would hurt. Would it be dull like a punch or more similar to a sharp sting? The longer it took for J to press the button, the worse the anxiety became. I was willing it to happen just to stop the waiting.

"I can't do it!" J said.

Stein rolled her eyes. "Yes, you can."

I heard J's breathing as if it were all around me, a hundred times closer and far, far slower. I found it soothing. I felt relaxed and started to focus on the sound before my body filled with a thump of pain that made me tense involuntarily and spasm. The button flew out of my hand on to the floor and my body tried to fold itself backwards.

It was over almost immediately.

J was looking at me, terrified that I had been badly hurt and repeatedly apologising. I realised the pain had come and gone, that it was just a single jolt of electricity and I could control myself again.

"How did that make you feel?" Stein asked J.

J didn't speak for a moment and then said softly, almost in a whisper, "Awful. I'm not doing it again."

Stein ignored J's response and suggested we did it the other way around.

J's head shook. Stein could see that I wasn't going to do it, so got up from her desk. She walked towards the grip with the button that I'd dropped on the floor and picked it up. She walked slowly back to her desk and balanced the cylindrical object upright in front of her. She looked carefully at it to make sure it would not fall and then turned her attention to us.

"Why won't you do it? You've just experienced pain, why should you suffer alone?"

"I don't understand the point in this. What is hurting one another going to achieve?" J said.

We heard the echoey clicks of hard shoes hitting the floors of the corridor as someone walked towards the room. Stein waited for the sound to begin to fade away and then picked up the button on her desk and started to examine it in both her hands.

She ignored J and spoke to me. "You're here because you want to be here. I haven't forced you to come?"

"No," I said.

"You know what we are trying to achieve, that's why you're here. You want to achieve it too, don't you?"

"Yes. But it's one thing to agree to hurt ourselves, what's the point in hurting one another?"

Stein held the switch between her thumb and forefinger and watched herself move it around, enjoying J's nervousness that I was no longer in control of it.

"We've spoken about pain. We've spoken about love. And we've spoken about how these things can be debilitating, haven't we?"

"Yes."

"Well, being debilitated can give us a window into reality. I want to see you both be debilitated. I want you to debilitate one another. It will help us to find a bridge into reality."

Stein put her thumb gently onto the button but didn't press it down.

"We can't have these sorts of discussions every time we do an experiment. If you knew how to experience reality, you wouldn't be here. But you are here. And the reason you're here is because you know I can help."

Stein took a deep breath. She moistened her lips with a small stroke of her tongue and looked over to J.

"I'm going to press this now and it is going hurt you. It's going to really hurt you."

J's pupils dilated, drowning out the colour in each eye. I was about to protest but before I could say a thing, Stein pressed the button and J's body erupted into frenzied convulsions.

I watched for a while, hoping it would end quickly. Stein looked on with a grotesque calmness. She began to smile as J lurched onto the floor from the seat.

"Stop!" I shouted at her but the button remained firmly pressed. I realised I had to stop what was happening. I could see smoke coming from J's skin and I leapt out of the chair to wrestle the switch from Stein's hand. My strength and coordination were still recovering from my shock and she easily avoided me, keeping the switch held down.

J was losing all bodily functions; the room began to smell putrid and still Stein kept the button pressed firmly down, her thumb turning white.

Again, I found myself watching J suffer horrifically without knowing what to do to stop it, absorbed completely in helplessness and panic.

Then the world started to change.

Suddenly, I felt a small comfort. I could see a wall of glorious colour forming over the room. I could see J's body regain control and from the torment emerged a soft smile. Our eyes met and we shared a faultless moment of shared understanding. We seemed to be sharing feelings I had never known existed, as though recognisable emotions were merged into one another to the point that they became separate, unique sensations. They were warming but also fleeting, lasting less than a second, but within that moment, I felt a remnant of the reality I'd experienced before. It felt like you were there, not just in your imagination but briefly part of the moment, part of J.

Normality was pushed out of the room as you filled it and then disappeared, making the room feel impossibly hollow in your absence. It became dark. I collapsed on to the floor and J burst into wild sobs. Stein dropped the button and ran quickly away from us and into the maze of corridors. It was the only time I'd see her act instinctively.

Everything was forgotten. The sobs became giggles and J started to laugh in the murky light of the oppressive room.

15.

It may seem strange to you that I was excited about what was happening. But I instinctively knew I was getting closer to you. Nothing else mattered any more. What I had seen and shared with J changed our perspective entirely.

We wanted more. More pain. More light. More glory.

J and I had been told that we should now stay at the institution full time. Stein was impressed by us and wanted to focus her attentions more fully on what we were capable of achieving. We were left alone together in a room with a few beds, some scattered machines and vapid pictures in frames made of cheap wood. We hadn't been waiting for long before the door swung open and a chorus of earnest voices entered, originating from a flurry of anonymous people in white clothes who went to work around us with a rousing urgency.

We were both helped out of our clothes and into hospital gowns in front of one another. The last time I had seen J in a state of such undress was the horrific day that led us to where we were now. I felt so ashamed about it that I fought my natural intrigue to look over.

Soon we were once again sitting in Stein's office, this time looking like patients in a hospital and buzzing with an electric belief that we could achieve the miraculous.

"Would you be more willing to hurt one another now that you know the sort of experience it can create?" Stein asked.

Neither of us wanted to be the first to answer. It felt strange to be enthusiastic about hurting a close friend, but it was clear now that we would. Happily.

Stein held the pause for an oddly long time. She smiled at both of us; it was the least genuine smile I have ever seen.

"We are part of a mind. We aren't real. We want to be, that's the reason you're both here, but we aren't."

It seemed like a strange thing to say. Purely factual. It was information we already knew and I got the sense that she had said it only because it was important that she started her explanation from a place of common understanding.

"Our only purpose is to play the parts that the mind wants us to play."

She stared at us to make sure we were following everything she was saying.

"And the most important one of us is the one who plays the part of the mind itself."

She was looking directly at me and I knew instantly she had discovered who I was.

"You aren't going to enjoy this." She looked searchingly at me and then moved her glare to J. "But I dare say it may be even worse for you."

I realised immediately what Stein was about say and the unspeakable damage that these words would cause.

"Would you like to tell J or should I?" She asked me.

I struggled to genuinely believe that she knew; I couldn't understand how it was possible. I searched my mind, running around it again and again. I became dizzy but I realised she couldn't possibly be talking about anything else.

I started to dread the inevitability of what was about to come, knowing there was no escape left. I couldn't hide anymore. There would be no more running from my crimes. I tensed against the fear of knowing I was about to be exposed until I became conscious of doing so and took back control. I started to relax. The anxiety of having to permanently conceal who I was and what I'd done began to disappear.

I felt J next to me. My wonderous J, who I adored. All the trust and love between us was about to vanish instantly. It felt unfair and for a brief moment I desperately searched again for a reason not to tell the truth. I hated myself. Every thought was confused and I wanted to stop time so that I had a chance to think clearly. But time continued and no inspiration came.

J sat there, still innocently unaware of what was about to be revealed. I was trembling. I didn't know how to formulate the words, my mind paralysed with shame.

"I think it's time J knew, don't you?" Stein said.

It was inevitable. I couldn't delay anymore and there was no alternative.

Stein was mimicking a ticking clock. "Tick. Tock. Tick. Tock"

"I'm so sorry," I said. I felt sick, so violently sick. I couldn't believe that this was happening. I wanted everything to end.

"Tell me what?"

"Come on, J," Stein said. "You're cleverer than that. Your friend here has been hiding quite the secret."

I knew that if I allowed Stein to tell J, I would lose control of how everything was explained. Stein would make it appear too simple, she would portray me as wholly evil. I had to tell J myself, I knew that. Only one second remained where I could look into J's eyes and see something other than the hate that I was about to put into them.

"I knew," I said with a pathetic, quivering voice. "I'm sorry. I was there and I knew it happened."

Stein continued to probe. "What else?"

I hated myself.

"I watched it." I heard the words but I didn't feel like I was saying them.

"You watched?"

"I don't know why. I am so sorry." But they were only thoughts. The words would not materialise. I was mute.

"What else?" Stein said.

All was already lost. The worst part was the easiest to say.

"You were raped in a dream that I created."

I was about to explain how sorry I was and how little control I had but Stein was getting impatient, and took over. She forced J to understand the horrendous details. That the rape only happened because I thought of it. That you were so disgusted by the thought you felt genuine guilt, disgust and horror. That your emotions became embedded within the dream and turned a thought into a real experience. That if it weren't for me, none of the pain and suffering J had endured would ever have happened.

Stein seemed to be enjoying herself more than any normal person would in such a situation, basking in my agony and J's slow understanding of my betrayal.

I turned so that my whole body faced J. My back was slouched. I was subservient, willing to do anything to fix what I had done, even though I knew it was impossible.

J wouldn't even look at me.

"Good," said Stein.

She looked at both of us cheerfully, sensing the horror in the room.

"The problem with being imaginary," Stein continued, speaking unnaturally slowly, "is that we really don't understand consequences. Reality is made from them. What you think is the worst thing that has ever happened to you is actually the closest to reality you have ever been. If you are sure that reality is what you want, you need to learn to embrace consequences."

Stein took the electric grips and buttons out from her desk. She tied the grips to our hands and gave us the buttons. We both passively allowed it to happen.

"Let's go back in time," Stein said.

J leaned forward, elbows on knees, staring contemplatively at the floor, trying to hide from the world. I could only glimpse part of a flushed cheek that I assumed was red with anger. I didn't think Stein would need to persuade J to press the button this time.

Stein made herself comfortable in her chair.

"This is what I suggest we do. Let's replay the entire experience. J, if you feel negative emotions, press the button and express these to your 'friend.'"

Stein looked at me. "If you feel that you are being punished too cruelly, take your revenge."

J stopped slouching and threw the button on the floor before glaring at me.

"Interesting," Stein said.

I saw a different version of my old friend. An older, more withered face, small dotted drops of sweat and a tightness, as if every muscle was being tensed at the same time.

I tried to comprehend J's anger and loneliness. I wanted J to hurt me. I deserved to be hurt. I needed to be made to suffer, I needed to feel like J had received justice and that I was paying my penance. I hadn't considered what J wanted. I said nothing.

"I've always felt it. You're a version of God, aren't you?" J asked me.

"No, it's not like that. I'm imaginary, just like you. I'm only a depiction of something real. I have no control."

"But you still created the dream?"

"I didn't mean to. I don't know how I did it, but…"

"But," interrupted Stein. "You could have stopped it and you didn't."

"You're an evil God," J said.

"I'm not. I don't mean to be. I can't stop this, don't you think I want to?"

"Don't compare this to a dream," said Stein. "You can always end a dream, you simply chose not to."

Stein stared sternly at me, confident that there could be no more argument. Then she changed form as only imaginary things can and moved into J's mind, becoming simply a voice and a presence. She spoke calmly but not normally from inside J's head, infecting the space where my depiction of J had been. Her words were whispered, cruelly, directly, into J's mind.

"Let's start as you enter the old hall. Only this time, you can remember your closest friend orchestrating everything from the window whilst you're shivering with fear."

I heard a pained, incoherent gasp of anger as though J had become possessed by a new knowledge about Stein that was unknown to me. I watched in amazement as J rejected Stein's presence and forced her back into her normal form before attacking her with extreme violence.

Stein anticipated the attack and called loudly for help but before it arrived J had pinned Stein to the floor, beating her with both hands.

Stein implored me to save her. I could have pressed the button in my hand and the voltage would have crashed through J, stopping all of this instantly. But I didn't want to. I felt inclined only to watch and to trust, entirely, J's instincts to hurt Stein.

When the help arrived, it was barbaric. Stein was swept away quickly, clutching at the wounds that J had inflicted. I was knocked over by the wave of responders and overheard an order bellowed from down the corridor. Everyone ran out of the room and a man entered in a chemical suit with a hose in his hands.

Then my memory fades. There was a moment after we were sprayed with the poison when we felt nothing but knew horror was on the way. When the pain took us, it was so intense that neither of us could do anything but scream until our voices gave up and then our bodies failed to draw breath, to think, to be. The agony was the only thing that existed. We writhed around the room in a fit, unconscious of everything but pain, its intensity increasing with every beat of our hearts.

Then, achingly slowly, the colourful light came and with it a joy and comfort that transcended everything.

That was when I felt you fully for the first time. I was alone with you. I had your complete attention. Everything I breathed was warmed, perfumed air. My skin tingled and I shuddered with an exquisite comfort. I was the universe, I was a god, I was part of everyone we both love. I was kindness, I was joy. I was covered with an addictive warmth. I was made aware of hidden anguishes and as they were shown to me, they evaporated away. I was confident. I was capable. I was everything I wished to be and everything that those I love want of me.

All that glory ended when the poison faded.

J's pain wasn't taken away like mine. I saw Stein watching us from a window outside the room, transfixed by J's agony. That was the last vision I had before I fell unconscious.

16.

I woke up days later in the room where J and I had been asked to stay in-between experiments. I immediately thought back to the joys I had experienced and wondered if I had once again become intertwined with part of reality. I mused upon it for a while until I remembered what had happened before the poison was sprayed on us like vermin.

I needed to see J. I didn't know what I would say. I would have said anything to fix this rupture and reset our friendship. I would have done anything to expel the dream from history. Stein had been right and the point annoyed me, you can always end a dream if you try hard enough. I hadn't stopped it back then and I hated myself for it now. I always had but I never knew how to express that properly to J. But at the time, I still didn't understand anything. I couldn't accept the full weight of my responsibility because I didn't feel as though I could control anything at all. In the world of the imagination, every consequence can be reimagined away. There is no truth because there is no permanence to anything other than the imagination itself. To feel reality seep in and pour consequence into the darkest thoughts I'd ever had felt like an intrusion. I started to feel more anger towards what had happened to J rather than guilt. I understood why it was my fault but I found it hard to feel responsible. I could never have known that reality and consequence had attached themselves to the dream. I could never have known J was really being hurt, or that I couldn't immediately reimagine a world where it never happened. I didn't realise then who I was or what I was capable of doing. A sense of overwhelming helplessness stuck with me during Stein's experiments. I had absolutely no control and yet knew that it was only because of me that anything happened at all.

When I felt some strength return, I sat up in the bed and wondered where J had gone. I heard footsteps approaching from the corridor outside and placed my feet on the cold floor. The door opened and Stein appeared. She walked towards me with purpose, a team in white coats following behind her. I knew immediately that one of them was an Arrow. He had a noticeable awareness of other things that were happening around us that nobody else could sense. He would constantly and quickly shift his gaze to an otherwise empty corner of the room, just as I had seen Philip do in the past. He also had confident walk and a fading form that made me think he was only partly present at any one time.

Stein moved a chair from under the window frame and then sat, with her notebook on her lap, watching her team moving around the room.

"I think that what happened before was a success, don't you?" Stein said.

"That was intentional?"

"Of course. Everything I do is intentional. Do you remember exactly what happened?"

"Yes," I said.

"What do you remember?"

"That you ruined my friendship…"

"Please. This is an experiment. Taking all of this personally will get us nowhere. What happened after that? When we sprayed you with the poison?"

"It *was* personal. You had absolutely no right."

"To tell J your secret or to spray you with poison?"

"Both."

Stein sighed deeply and beckoned one of her entourage with a flick of her wrist.

"Get water. Maybe food?" She looked at me, her head turned sideways. I shook my head. "Just water then," she added.

We watched as it was poured from a plastic container at the rear of the room then brought to me.

"Now," Stein said, confident that ordering someone else to do me a basic favour would allow us to move on from past indiscretions. "Forget the methods. They are for me to understand."

I drank my water.

"I would not be doing any of this if it wasn't necessary," she continued, her eye brows raised and lips tightly pressed together.

"Forget the methods," she repeated. "The results are the only things that are important. Do you remember the result?"

"Yes."

"Tell me about it. How did you feel during the experience?"

I paused to reflect on the intensity of the sensation.

"Agony. It was agony and it was all-consuming. I couldn't... I couldn't focus on anything but the pain and then it was gone. It was as though it was pumped out of me in one moment of violence, like being hit. And then everything changed and all the pain left and became happiness. But not imaginary happiness, it felt real. Just as the dream felt real. I saw J before it went dark. I saw that the pain had not been taken away like it was for me. It ruined the last moments. Then I can't remember anything."

I stared at the wall over Stein's shoulder and dwelt on the experience and the oddness of all that had happened since I'd met her. She was taking notes as I spoke. I peered over to see what she was writing but it was illegible.

"Where is J?"

Stein finished writing.

"We need to do it again. Now."

"What?"

"We need to give you more poison."

I instinctively shifted backwards.

"When you came into contact with the poison, we saw a light, pulsing into you. We need to see it again." Stein nodded as if she were trying to force me to follow suit. "We need to analyse what it is. To do that we need you to have more poison."

I thought back to the light and wondered what it was. I allowed myself to believe it might be a gateway to you. Or some sort of representation of you, outside of me. I was intrigued. I forgot the pain the poison caused; I remembered the joy.

A woman stepped forward and motioned to the bed. I lay back on to it and Stein had a bottle of the green liquid brought towards me. She put on gloves and began to unscrew the top.

"A drop. On your tongue."

I was breathing heavily, holding tightly on to the sheets of the bed with both hands.

Stein extracted some of the liquid with a pipette and looked at me, expecting some acknowledgement of what she was about to do. Her team moved around with strange equipment on wheeled tables and surrounded me. I felt a leather strap tied onto my legs and saw a larger one being attached to the body of the bed, ready to be tied around my waist. They had been practicing. It only took a few seconds for me to be completely restrained and everyone to take their place.

Stein walked forward carefully holding the green liquid.

"Open your mouth."

The liquid was carefully placed upon my tongue. I felt two drops that thudded with an unnatural heaviness and then immediately dissolved into me. Stein walked backwards, carefully taking off her gloves. I anticipated the pain that was on its way and by doing so, I made myself more sensitive to even the tiniest of sensations.

It tingled first, a slight vibration originating from the extremities of my body and building with intensity until it entered my head. Then the horror came. I recognised it now and tried to fight against it. I told myself to ignore how it felt, to focus on what would come next but it battled through all my superficial defences. I began tugging violently on the straps, twisting and screaming to get away. I kicked my legs violently and writhed around because any stillness seemed to be punished acutely. Hold on, I screamed to myself. Hold on!

Then came the thud, a deep, single pound into me and the pain left, ushering in a blissful sense of relief with a building happiness and warmth. I was away from this world, entering somewhere perfect and pure. A place that mattered, a place where I was wanted, a place where you knew me and loved me as I love you.

Then it all faded away like a sound into the atmosphere, leaving me shivering as I became once again conscious of the room. Stein's team were undoing my shackles and packing away their things.

"You should try to get some more rest," Stein said. "We will need to spend some time analysing the findings. Stay here, don't go anywhere."

"Did you see the light?" I asked.

Stein was waiting for the others to leave the room, gesturing for them to move quicker.

"Yes. We saw it." She shut the door behind her, returning me to silence and boredom.

I began to daydream about what had just happened. Lying on the bed, I tried to recreate the joy I'd felt but I couldn't sense it any longer. A connection had been severed and I became less sure of what I was chasing, as though woken abruptly from a beautiful dream and left only with the lingering awareness of a dwindling delight. Even the memory of the feeling became too obscure to sense and I couldn't focus on anything but the mundane surroundings of the room.

I paced up and down, becoming increasingly anxious about seeing J again and what I would say. In my head, I was constantly challenging what Poppy had made me believe. If it was my world, why would I have created it like this? Why would I be in the position that I was in? Why would I have made someone, even subconsciously, so perfect and then destroy my friendship with them?

The extraordinary oddness of Stein also made no sense. I hadn't contemplated any of this, the world was moving too quickly for me to consider anything other than Stein's peculiar experiments and methods. Now that I was alone and with time, I could once again consider the improbability of what Poppy had told me. Her words started feeling less true, even though a deep conviction constantly stopped me from acknowledging she might be wrong.

I was anxious about seeing J. I tried calling out but there was no reply and I assumed J didn't want to see me. I asked the next person I saw if I could be taken to where J was. They told me I'd have to wait and for hours nobody came. Eventually one of Stein's team emerged.

"I'll take you now."

I was led through the endless corridors and in a lift to a vault deep below the building. The longer our route became through the monumental structure, the more my curiosity grew until it turned into a searing panic and I wanted to move faster and faster to wherever I was being taken.

"Where are we going?" I remember asking. And then, "What's wrong, why is J here?"

"We're nearly there," said the man in the white coat leading the way. His words were said nervously, as though he had been told to say nothing at all.

A large metal door was pushed open with obvious effort and squeaked loudly. Beyond was a dimly lit room with a metal table in the middle. On that table was J.

J's body was gaunt and rubbery. I stared for a while at J's lifeless remains. I couldn't stop. I felt myself shake and become dizzy, wrapping my fingers around the edges of the table to keep my balance.

Small surges of rage made me search for someone to confront but then dwindled almost instantly. There was no longer anyone there but me. I looked at J and had an urge to scream but suppressed these urges because I knew they would achieve nothing. I tried to convince myself that what I was seeing was impossible. Imaginary people can't die. I would never create this world, why would I? I searched my mind for a reason but every thought was interrupted by the horrific permanence of the image in front of me.

I turned to leave and walked through the corridors then decided for no reason that I needed to run back. I was finding it hard to breathe. I became more curious, more aware of what was actually happening. A slow sadness began to wash everything else away, surging like a tide from nowhere but filling everything with its presence.

I moved slowly towards the body and carefully placed my hand on J's head. Visions of who we once were swam around the room. I felt the tingles on my back again, the softness of the kisses, the goosepimples, caresses and sweet kindness that used to stream so naturally and generously from something immeasurably different to what lay in front of me.

J's life was so much more than the memories that had been left, these pictures taken from afar, vague silhouettes of what was everything. They could never represent the colour and wonder of what had been lost, my source of sacred joys, the subtle glances as we walked together, the gentle hand clasped by my own, that secret smile within a crowd.

A warm tear rolled down my cheek and onto J. I said nothing but begged for forgiveness. For a moment the room was a shrine, J lying amidst flowers and candles whilst a lone voice sang and I knelt at the feet of the divine. But that moment passed quickly. I was returned to silence and I sat upon the cold floor of the oppressive room, a vault of helpless sorrow, immersed in sadness, endlessly longing for the J I once knew.

17.

The following days were full of bitter memories. I wandered around every part of our mind to find them, pick them up and replay them. I went to the fields where J first emerged into the world. I returned to the hidden clearings in the woods where we first touched each other and to the parallel world where we learned to love. I never wanted the clarity of J's memory to fade. All the thoughts were so wonderfully happy but each one was spoilt by flashing images of J vulnerable, naked, violated and shuddering with fear. I could remember the shocking evil of the scene; the way it always tormented me, a picture of divine sensuality within the cellars of hell. It corrupted all the happiness we had shared.

I'd failed to protect J. Twice. I felt horribly inadequate and frustrated by my own limitations. I'd let J down. I was so sorry. I am so sorry.

I thought of you in the world of the real where consequences steer your every move. How I admired you, your ability to cope with your mistakes and live within such severe physical dimensions. How you effortlessly seem to savour moments and then let them go. Death was new to me; as were consequences. My mistakes and inadequacies clung to me viciously and made me miserable. They stifled me, I could do nothing but dwell upon them. I wished I could be more like you. I'm sure the agony of J's death and Stein's experiments affected you too. Maybe a stinging headache or a few weeks of melancholy. Nothing too serious, just an awareness that something felt wrong. It was.

Eventually I began to realise I couldn't preserve the memories of J with the clarity I wanted. They started fading away, blending into emptiness like ghosts into the night. I frantically searched everywhere J had ever been for a sign of life but always returned to Stein's institution where I waited on more news and hoped that some goodness, some greater understanding of who we were, of reality, of meaning, would give some purpose to J's sacrifice.

Neither J or Stein were anywhere to be found. My sadness and desperation drove to me into a heavy tiredness and eventually I stopped searching for J. Instead, I sat in my room deep within Stein's institution, waiting for news, or for someone to tell me what to do next.

My friends visited. I had avoided them at first, terrified by the judgement I thought they would pile upon me. As visitors, they could only come to an extravagantly decorated common room above the main hall of the building. It had grandiose portraits, presumably of those who had founded the institution and launched it towards its current prestige. There was a large stone fireplace flanked by enormous windows that looked out on to the streets which meandered through the city beyond. It was a freezing but terrifyingly still day, ice wrapping every piece of the ground in a deceptively clear sheet. The fire struggled valiantly to chase away the chill and we sat in the leather chairs that had been huddled around it.

For a while we said nothing, enjoying the familiar company and unable to express, in any substantive way, the loss that we shared.

"I'm so sorry," I said.

"It's not your fault," C told me. "How could it be?"

Alice sat next to me and held my hand. "C's right, dear. Don't blame yourself, it will achieve nothing."

"How does something like this even happen?" asked Philip. "People don't die. They can't. This isn't the real world. J must still be here somewhere."

"If that was true, you of all people would know, wouldn't you?" Alice asked Philip.

"That's why it's so troubling. J is nowhere. It makes no sense. It's as if even the memories are without any substance." He looked at me. "What exactly has been happening here?"

I longed to explain everything I knew. I suspected they may soon realise themselves what I was trying to hide. Reality was taking over our world. I wondered how much longer I could pretend to be just another innocent observer.

"They play with pain. Sometimes they give us a green liquid which hurts but then it takes us somewhere…" I remembered the perfection of the moments. "Somewhere beautiful, somewhere that feels closer to reality. It takes us out of the imagination for a while. It causes consequences. As though it can change things within the imagination permanently."

"A green liquid?" Alice said. "Like a poison?"

"It *is* poison."

"They're poisoning you?" C asked. The Arrow I had noticed when I last saw Stein fluttered in and out of the room.

"I'm not allowed to talk about any of this."

"Are you sure you want to be here?" asked Alice.

"Yes. It sounds like madness, I know, but something extraordinary is happening."

Alice glanced over at the others, then her eyes flicked back to me. "Did the poison kill J?"

"Yes. I think so, anyway. It must have been the poison."

"You shouldn't be here," Alice replied dismissively. "This is not worth risking another life over. Philip, why are the Arrows allowing something like this to happen?"

"I don't know. But I'm going to find out."

I nearly tried to defend Stein and her methods but I stopped myself. I couldn't understand what was happening either, though I knew they would feel differently if they realised who I was and how extraordinarily close we were to something I couldn't explain but which felt so significant.

"Have either of you heard of anything like this happening before?" C asked Philip and Alice.

"No."

"Well, doesn't that tell you something about how extraordinary this place is? Anything that pushes boundaries is bound to create suffering and pain." C stood up and walked towards the fire place then looked back at me. "I think that what you are doing is about the bravest thing I have ever heard."

Philip leant forward on his seat. "What is wrong with you? One of our greatest friends has died. Why are you are defending those responsible? I, personally, preferred it when permanent death was only something that could happen in reality, didn't you?"

"I'm not defending the place, merely what has been achieved."

"And what is that?"

"Well, something that you just admitted has never been achieved before."

"Please don't argue," I said. I didn't want their opinions. I wanted their friendship and support, even if I wasn't sure I was still worthy of it.

Philip shook his head. "I need to find out more about this place."

"Yes, you do," Alice agreed before turning her attention to me. "And you need to consider very carefully what you're doing here. If we lose you as well, what sort of achievement is that?"

I placed my head in my hands and rubbed my temples with my fingers. I looked at the floor and saw the individual threads of the carpet intricately wrapped together in shades of colours I'd never consciously considered. I glanced at Alice and then Philip. I saw his silhouette against the bright light coming through the window. I changed my focus and saw the haphazard roofs and walls of the buildings beyond. Some were made of a greyish slate that I knew nothing about, others with a pinkish tile that I recognised but felt no connection with. Back in the room, I hated aspects of the décor, the weird patterns on the carpets and the furniture which lacked any character. Everything was a mix of objects that I would never select, put together in a way that I did not believe I was capable of conceiving. My eyes marvelled at the mesmerising allure of C. A fantasy too extraordinary for my creativity alone to have been able to achieve.

"You are part of our God, my child." Poppy's words were swirling around my head. It felt too unbelievable, everything I was seeing and experiencing was outside of me. But it was undoubtedly true. There was a reality that had seeped into my experiences and changed the very structure of the imagination. It could not occur without me and, as unbelievable as it seemed, I knew I had to start believing fully. I embraced the truth that Poppy had told me in a way I hadn't before and it made me want to contemplate its meaning. I didn't really want to talk anymore, I wanted to be alone.

"I know what you think of all of this," I told Alice. "But I can't stop. This is where I need to be."

C came over and took my hand. "I know how much this means to you. We are always here. Always. I'll come back if you ever need me."

Alice sighed and shook her head. "This needs to stop. It needs to stop now."

"It doesn't," I said. "J's life has to be worth something."

"And how will carrying on with this insanity achieve that? You're chasing the impossible. I can't lose you too. I won't! This needs to stop."

Alice stood as if to leave, looking down at me and willing me to follow her out.

"No," I said. "It needs to carry on. I won't leave."

Alice searched Philip for support. He nodded, letting her know that it was there.

"She's right," he said. "It's madness for you to stay. At least until I can find out more about what this place is. Come on, let's go."

I knew I wasn't going to leave. I was sad and lonely. I was no longer enjoying the comfort of having these familiar faces around me. I wished Alice and Philip could be more supportive, like C. But I couldn't make it happen. I didn't know how. I only knew that I wasn't going to leave and they would never force me.

"I'm staying. I know what you are saying makes sense to you. But if you had seen what I have seen, you would understand."

Alice was about to speak but was immediately cut off by C. "The decision has been made. It's not a time to argue, just try to support the decision."

Alice was shaking her head with small, subtle movements as she came over and placed her hand on my shoulder in a reluctant display of friendship and support. Then she left.

C kissed my forehead and followed Alice out of the grand doors. As Philip was about to leave, he turned back to me.

"How long have the Arrows been here?"

"Since the last experiment."

He nodded disapprovingly, then followed Alice and C into the bitter cold outside.

I returned to my room and pictured J sitting on the bed only days before when we were waiting nervously between experiments. We were both so excited, slowly becoming aware of the potential of what we were doing.

J is just something I created. The room is something I created. This is the imagination. I repeated the words to myself, saying it aloud, addressing the empty space where J once sat. Then I curled into the bed, covering myself completely with the sheets and hid from everything. I screamed into the pillow, again and again, until I was exhausted. Then I began to weep uncontrollably, my mind reaching out to J, hopelessly, until I lost consciousness.

18.

My resolve to live as though I were genuinely in control of my own world meant that Stein now frightened me less. I had been furious with her, realising that she had intentionally kept J's death from me so that she could do another experiment. Even afterwards, she had ignored me and then reluctantly asked an anonymous member of her team to show me J's body. She had still offered no explanation, avoiding me completely and refusing to confront anything that had happened. But I needed to start realising that it wasn't Stein who had done any of those things. It was me. My anger was fruitless. I needed to live the truth and stop allowing myself to believe that everyone had a mind of their own.

Having vanished for three days, Stein now demanded my presence in her office. This time, for the first time ever, we were completely alone. Stein offered no sympathy, it was not something she could naturally muster but there were signs that she understood my loss. She spoke of my sadness and was clearly surprised when I told her that I wanted to continue with more experiments immediately.

"So quickly?"

"Yes, let's get on with it. There's no point wallowing in self-pity."

Stein raised her eyebrows and then lowered her eyes to look at her notes. She sighed away her interest that I was so keen to push things forward and then returned to her normal self.

"You feel sad?" she asked me.

"Yes, of course I feel sad."

"Tell me how it hurts?"

"Why?"

"Because it might be useful."

"How?"

"Stop it. These questions are unhelpful. Pain causes a connection with reality, you know this. Tell me about your pain so that I can see if it can be used to help achieve something."

"Did the last experiment achieve anything? You can't carry on hiding all this information from me and expect me just to do whatever it is you come up with next."

Stein allowed her head to fall sideways. "I could expect that from you if I wish." She paused again, looking directly at me and tapping one finger slowly on her desk. "We analysed the light. It's not something that we have seen before, it has properties that are more similar to a force. It's therefore something that we need to explore."

She paused for a long time, expecting me to wait until she spoke again and to display that she had taken control of the conversation. It was a behaviour that I had come to expect.

"I have nothing else to tell you," she added. I admired her calmness and effortless authority. I started to realise that all her strengths were things that I had gifted her.

"Please tell me more about how it hurts."

I ignored the question. I couldn't explain the pain and I thought it irrelevant. I wanted to get more information from her.

"How did you realise who I was?" I asked.

Stein's eyes temporarily darted around the room and then back to me. I could tell she was uncomfortable.

"It was obvious," she replied.

"How was it obvious?"

"Because J could not have experienced anything resembling reality unless you were you."

"Have you considered what that means? Me being who I am?"

"How do you mean?"

"I mean, you would not exist if I had not invented you. You would not know who I was unless I had allowed you to have that information first."

Stein cackled and then appeared to relax slightly. She pinched the corners of a small stack of paper on her desk between her thumb and index finger so that each sheet became perfectly aligned.

"You are hardly in control. If you were, why would you be here? Why would you allow me to hurt you? Why would you have created me at all?"

"Because I need you to help me find a way to become real."

Once the pile of paper had been perfectly aligned, she moved it to the side of her desk, ensuring that the edges of the paper were parallel to the edges of the desk.

"There is no purpose to what you do. You may be the creator but you are not in control of your creations." Stein lent forward and faked a smile. "And you know it."

Then she stood, walked around the table to where I was sitting and slapped me in the face.

"Otherwise, what possible reason would there be for me doing that?"

I jumped up, about to hit back but stopped myself. I felt pathetic. Stein calmly moved back to her seat.

"You are not my master. You create. I'll be in control. I want you to tell me how J's death is hurting you and I want you to be as specific as possible."

Silence. I was contemplating everything once more. Creation and control, such different concepts and yet surely you are in control of what you create? I felt the fabric of my clothes against my body, the weight of myself upon the chair. I could smell the sterile tinge of antiseptic in the room. I kept telling myself it was mine. Stein was not Stein, she was just an image that I was constantly creating. I tried to accept it but every outward sense was telling me that it wasn't true.

"What do you know about pain?" I asked. If Stein was a part of me, I would make her useful. She clearly knew things I was hiding from myself.

"I know everything there is to know about pain. I have made it my business. There is nothing that you can tell me that I will not be able to understand." Stein leant back, breathed with a slight self-satisfaction and waited for me to speak again.

I was inviting myself, through Stein, to learn more.

"The pain I get from missing J is completely different to the pain from the poison. It is everywhere, all the time. It never wears off and follows me like a shadow. It kills any happiness but is always light enough to be carried. The poison bites and rips. It strips everything away and cannot be tolerated, like being engulfed in flames. The two are worlds apart but equally powerful."

"Does it stop you from thinking? Does it debilitate you?"

"Not completely. It's patient. It lingers, interrupting thoughts and hanging on to them as they come and go. When I'm not doing anything, it fills the void completely."

"Have you ever felt anything like it before?"

"No. I've never felt sadness or loss like this. It's impossible, all emotions are just imagined. Loss can never be overwhelming, people can die and come back infinitely but this time something is completely different. There is nothing left of J at all. Even the memories seem to be deteriorating impossibly fast. There is no essence left anywhere, I can't even imagine being with J. I can't find J, even the Arrows can't sense any part of anything J used to be. It is as if J has died in reality, not in the imagination."

"Which Arrows have you been talking to?" Stein asked immediately.

"Yours." I lied. "The one that you have brought to the experiments."

Stein smiled and leant forward, picking up her pen and writing franticly.

"You just lied," she said, putting the pen down again and looking up at me. "You need to get better at this. You're far too transparent."

"What does that mean?"

"It means that you are unable to mislead anyone. It's a major concern because if everyone realises who you are, it will be very difficult to protect you. The power of creation is a dangerous companion. People will do anything to get what they want from you."

"But I can't control what I create."

"Well, yes. Obviously. But I doubt others will believe you have as little control as you say."

Stein's attention turned to a tiny spot on her desk. She licked her thumb and rubbed at it aggressively before wiping it again with her middle finger. She looked back up at me with remnant of a snarl.

"You said that it felt as though J has died in reality. Has anything else happened since our experiments that has changed the imagination?"

I thought carefully. "No, all the changes are related to J. And they are huge changes. Nobody ever dies with such permanence. I've never seen memories fade so quickly and become inaccessible. It feels as though the rules of reality have taken over J."

"When you consider J, can you relate any of the feelings with those that you experience with the poison?"

"Yes. Everything about J's death has started to feel real. Consequential. Completely different to everything else *except* the poison."

Stein looked down at her desk for a while and pursed her lips.

"Yes," she said. "Yes, this is exactly what I expected."

She stood up, taking her notebook with her and went to the door. She left me for a couple of seconds before returning. Then she sat back down on her side of the desk and got comfortable again.

"We will do another experiment now. It will be unpleasant for you but I think that the conditions are perfect. You can create very close connections with reality when we use the poison and very weak but sustained connections when experiencing emotional pain. We need to use this emotional pain to provide a platform for further study."

A team started to come into the room. A seat with restraints was wheeled in, as was a large drip, some monitors and equipment that I recognised from the previous experiment. The team began to set everything up and the Arrow emerged from the doorway, the only one not wearing a white coat. He moved over to the side of the office and stared out of the window as the activity continued around us.

"Sit down on this seat," said Stein gesturing to the chair with restraints.

"What is going to happen?"

"I'll explain, sit first."

I'm creating this. I am creating this. I thought of Philip and Alice. The fury they would feel if they knew what I was doing. It would have been justified. As I moved towards the chair, I was walking towards torture. But I needed to start believing in who I was.

I sat and my arms and legs were restrained. The drip was brought over and Stein had two people move her seat so that it was closer to me.

"You need to consider J's loss at the same time as you feel the poison. It won't be pleasant but it will mean that you are taken completely away from the imagination and are only experiencing things that we know are connected to reality."

I resigned myself to the discomfort that was about to come and believed that I was capable of doing something extraordinary. I tried to forget J as they placed the drip into my arm. I tried to focus only on you, my destination, my ambition, my destiny.

Before the poison was allowed to drip into my veins Stein was handed a few things by the Arrow, just out of my sight. She went behind her desk and pressed a button. Music started to come out of speakers hidden in the ceiling. I recognised the beautiful songs immediately as those that I had listened to with J in our secret world. The enchanted melodies breathed life back to the glowing embers of the memories of J that I was losing, each glorious note delivering another thump of loneliness.

Stein studied my reaction and then nodded to someone behind me. I heard the click of a switch and on the wall in front of me, a cycle of images appeared. I looked at them to see J's saintly form staring back at me from all of the places where we had hidden ourselves away together.

With every image, a bitter sadness increased within me, amplifying the overwhelming magnitude of my loss. I sensed J everywhere, the untouchable, untenable presence of something that once exponentially increased happiness but now could only wound.

Stein placed something over my mouth and nose. I felt it first, the quickly fading coolth of something comfortingly soft. Then I smelt it and immediately knew it was something J had worn, the unmistakable smell still faintly recognisable but vanishing, constantly being diluted by time. I managed, for just a moment, to hold on to the most delicate of feelings that J was still somewhere around me, still filling space, breathing and being. But like every part of J, it quickly floated away, leaving emptiness behind.

I felt the material being pushed tightly against my nose and mouth, then clamped in place tightly with tape, so that I could hardly breath. I started to panic and then felt the heaviness of the poison entering my veins and prepared myself for the pain that was on its way.

It sliced into me violently. It was a torture that both humiliated and stung, as though I had been crucified and then set alight whilst my psychotic enemies danced happily around my melting body, watching me die, knowing that the last sight I would see was their triumphant faces. It wasn't just physical, my emotions were evaporating, burning out of existence and protesting against their end by spreading crippling agony through my body.

I heard Stein say something to me, I have no idea what, nothing made sense. Then I wasn't in pain anymore. There was nothing pleasant either, just a slight discomfort that I couldn't process because my mind no longer worked. I couldn't focus or think or move any part of my body. Then I couldn't see and I closed in on myself. I started to feel panic because I felt trapped but couldn't react to it. It was as if an obscure imposter had taken control of me. Time stopped and I became nothing. Nothing at all. I was vanishing.

For a while there was no time and no space. I drifted, nothing but a consciousness with nothing to sense but itself. It was comforting and I felt the comfort increase gradually until I was hit by a crashing wave of delight, floating in my own universe, joined by you and creating only greater and greater joys.

As the comfort had built, so too it began to fade. The new world where you and I were alone developed clear dimensions and then pushed itself away from us. A barrier emerged between us and everything that was there only moments before started to speed away, accelerating until it was indecipherable from the nothingness.

Then I began to sense once again. There was an expanse of which I was part. I felt something itch but I didn't know what it was and then suddenly I recognised it as a feeling. And then it was everywhere, like I was being bitten by tiny insects all over my body. It became unbearable but it was bringing me out of the darkness.

There was a thud. A heavy thud. Then another. I inflated. I realised I'd taken a breath and that it was the first time I'd remembered to do so for a while.

I could see again. There were colours but they were meaningless. Then, gradually, I began to sense what everything meant. I could see Stein but that didn't mean anything until I remembered who she was. Everything returned and my body felt angry and bruised.

I felt myself abandoned and in agony. I prepared for the end before a powerful shot of pressure blew into the room and smashed everything apart. It threw me away from the drip, which crashed against the opposite wall and sprayed the green poison all over the room, creating chaos and sending everyone screaming into the endless corridors that now echoed with shouts of horror.

I no longer wanted my body, it was a source of permanent pain. Nothingness came again and I embraced it.

19.

There is an intensity to extreme pain that memory can't mimic. I would never have allowed Stein to come near me with her poison again had I been able to remember how much it hurt. But I did forget eventually, I always did. I suffered gladly and suffering always increases resolve, even if the cause is madness. When your ambitions have caused loved ones to die, it becomes almost impossible to turn your back on what you have been striving for. To do so would be admitting that all the suffering had no purpose. It would immediately corrupt the meaning behind all of your actions, making them appear reckless rather than glorious. With each additional hardship, it becomes more natural to believe that one day all the suffering will be justified. I know this because it was what happened to me.

I believed that J's death was part of a great struggle to become more than imaginary. I became trapped in the stubbornness that suffering brings and captivated by the poison. Nobody could have saved me from Stein and I never considered giving up on what we were doing.

I didn't know what had happened after the chaos of the last experiment but consequences that could only be linked to that moment started to seep into the ever-changing world. I was lying on my bed once again in my characterless room when I became vaguely aware of a noise, a slow chant and a monotone horn. In my daze I felt at sea and thought it was a fog horn, calling out to me from the safety of the shore. But the pitch was too high and it was being blown in unequal bursts.

I sat up, straining against the aches of my exhausted body and looked out of the window at the streets below. The noises began to make sense. The streets were crammed with people and placards. Arrows stood with their arms crossed watching but not interfering until localised pockets of violence erupted.

I squinted to read one of the placards.

God is calling us.

I saw a group of people, lying on the road and chained together. They were being protected by burly men from onslaughts of violence from others in the crowd. They all wore white shirts with blood or paint splattered on to them. A massive flag was being flown nearby with the message

No torture is for the greater good.

There seemed to be one main march moving past my window that was separate from the static crowds in the smaller streets that hurled rocks and abuse at them.

In my room, the handle of the door startled me and I shot around to see who it was, considering for a moment that the violence had flooded into the building while I was staring out the window. When I turned, I found a woman with a kind face, who brought with her a meal and a change of clothes. I sighed with relief.

"What happened to everyone?" I asked her.

"Sorry, I can't talk to you."

She looked at me as she spoke and then lingered for a moment, as though uncertain about her behaviour. Then she placed the food on the table.

"What are they protesting about?"

She stopped what she was doing for a while and then turned back to me. She breathed in, as if preparing to speak but deciding against it. In silence she walked over to one of the other beds.

"Here's a change of clothes."

She left and I heard her steps vanishing down the corridor away from me, faster and less consistent than they should have been. They were soon drowned out by the noise from the crowds outside that reverberated constantly with sounds of anger. Within the ordered chants, there were distant screams of terror and then I felt a dull vibration, as if something heavy had fallen in the distance.

I had an urge for comfort, to hide from the outside and surround myself with something else. I slid under the sheets, moving my feet to the coldness of the corners of the bed and enjoyed the dark. The noise was undeterred but I felt somehow separated and safe behind my new, flimsy barrier. I had allowed my mind to wonder away for a time, but then it was stolen back by a stinging sensation on my foot. I immediately thought I'd been bitten and leapt out of the bed, expecting to see some small creature crawl out of the sheets. I couldn't see anything, so I ripped off the cover and spread it over the floor to make sure was nothing in it. As I did, my foot started to pulse with a dull ache and I became worried that something more serious was happening. I sat on the floor and studied my foot for any sign of a bite but the pain seemed to have no centre and I found it hard to know where to look. I was becoming increasingly uncomfortable, unable to focus on anything but the increasing intensity of the pain when, as quickly as it had come, it started to leave. My foot started to feel light and simply owning it contented me. It was as though something invisible was massaging it and easing out a tension that I hadn't realised was there.

Soon everything had returned to normal and I looked beyond my foot to see the sheet crumpled on the floor. There was a green stain on one of the corners. I moved towards it on my hands and knees, looking closer at the mark, eventually getting close enough to smell it. There was another scream outside, this time louder than all the others but somehow less troubling because I was so immersed in what I was doing. The smell, so different to any other, made me positive that the stain was the poison. It had the same rancid, bitter odour but there was also something sweet about it, like syrup on a rotting corpse.

I picked up the sheet so that the poisonous corner drooped towards the floor, safely away from my hands and took it back to the bed. Outside, there was the sound of glass smashing and loud cheers. I remember acknowledging it but no longer caring, the dark green stain had mesmerised me. Even as a single drop, the poison seemed to hold its power. It was uncompromised, undiluted, its ability to harm and comfort both perfectly intact. I was in awe of it. The pattern of the stain was so ordered. It did not resemble any normal liquid. Instead, it was as though the poison was alive, in control of its own borders, uncorrupted by other objects. A solid disguised as a liquid.

Without thinking, I grabbed the corner of the sheet and held it to my chest. Then I lay down on top of it, putting all of my weight on to the hand that held the stain. I prepared for onset of the pain and as it started, I forced myself not to move, to hold on for as long as it took to get the comfort.

The pain started to build while the noises of the crowds and the violence boomed outside. As the pain intensified, I screamed inwardly, forcing my hand to remain clamped shut.

Slowly the relief came. The pain retreated and now I clasped the sheet in my hand like it was sacred, forcing all of the joy I could out of it, getting up and wandering around the room in a daze. The chants outside became songs, the violence became passion. I was in love with where I was, I was in love with Stein. I was on my way to you.

The daze was fleeting. I returned to normality and the terror outside began to disturb me again. I opened my hand and could see that the poison had vanished, sucked from the sheet into my skin. I let the sheet drop on to the floor and lay back on the bed.

I focused for a while on the shouts and horns being blown outside, but my attention shifted quickly to a sudden itch that I hadn't felt before. I started to tingle everywhere and I realised that I needed something very urgently. The food that had been left was unappetising and the normality of the room was making me irritable. There seemed to be something incredibly important missing. I needed it desperately but I didn't know what it was, I was just certain that I'd realise when I found it.

I started to look in the various cupboards within the room. They were all empty. I searched under the beds and the small hollows between the walls and furniture. Eventually I had to leave the room because nothing in there was right.

I tried the next room and then the next until eventually, three doors down, I saw a locked cupboard and instinctively I realised what I was looking for.

I wanted the poison.

I couldn't cope without it. Even the thought of the pain, the gateway to happiness, was seducing me.

I took a chair and hit the lock on the cabinet as hard as I could, smashing it with the chair leg until it was ripped away. I opened the cupboard door, possessed with this new urge and took the lone bottle of green liquid that stood within it. I ran back to my room, hiding the bottle under my clothes and picked up the sheet, pouring a couple of drops on to it, then immediately clasping it with my hand. I waited. I got what I wanted but the joy was an anti-climax.

I needed more, so next I poured the poison on to my hand in a rush and half the bottle spilt all over my skin and the sheets. In a moment of terror, I put the bottle down and ran away from it, knowing that soon I would be in too much pain to control myself. I grabbed a pillow, stuffing as much as I could into my mouth so my screams could not be heard and waited for the suffering to begin. But I was getting better at dealing with the pain now. I could think my way through it and to the comfort, even though it seared through my body and relentlessly attacked every nerve.

I was more aware than normal when the comfort came and I thought I heard you speaking to me, asking me to prolong the comfort and stay with you. I became immersed in two worlds, one of horror where the violence outside boomed and my body was in constant agony and the other in my mind where I felt your presence and was happy.

I managed to mesmerise myself in this perfect state until the poison had all seeped into me. I returned to normal, bitterly disappointed and determined to return to the perfect harmony I'd been able to create.

I ran over to the unappealing tray of cold food. I took the spoon and poured as much liquid as it would hold.

As I moved it to my mouth, the door opened and Stein ran towards me, pushing my arm and spilling poison onto the floor. The splatter landed on both of us and for a brief moment she was furious. She knew she would feel the agony soon and shortly, she was squirming on the floor, trying to push through her own torment until the pain faded away. I stood and watched, better able to cope with the poison's acute sting. Stein's yelps merged with those of the crowd outside. I felt powerful as I stood over her. Then, as the pain faded, I slung open the window and embraced the passion, the energy, the glory of the crowds outside.

I had an awareness that Stein was behind me. That her suffering was ending and soon I would be facing the consequences of my actions. I closed my eyes to savour the last moments before I was pulled violently from the window, back in to the room and roughly pinned onto the bed.

The poison faded away and I slowly emerged back into myself, back into the room, away from you and away from happiness.

I became conscious only of the persistent pain in my head, Stein's breathing and the undecipherable chants of the crowds outside. I felt a shadow. Stein was standing over me.

"Never do that again."

I tried to focus on her.

"But I need it. I need it."

"No, you don't. Can you hear the crowds? Can you hear how important this is becoming? Can you see how little anything else matters?"

I nodded.

"Don't. Ruin. This."

20.

I know you have drugs in the real world too. There are some that cause such delight that they can make you feel invincible and then, when the effects start to fade, all of the pain that you felt before returns, worse than it was before. Instinctively you crave the drug again, take more and more, each time damaging yourself further. The deadly circle continues until you can't live with it or without it.

Poison had become my drug. The pain came first. Every time I used the poison, my body started to fight back against me, devising ways of making the misery I felt worse. It was trying to change my behaviour, to stop me from hurting myself but I knew I just had to wait. If I waited, then part of reality, part of you, would come and make me forget that it ever hurt.

Stein knew I had become an addict. She decreed that all poison be placed in a secure vault, guarded by Arrows. I reacted with a desperation that only increased everyone's resolve to protect me from myself. I frantically searched everywhere for a bottle or the forgotten remnants of the liquid that may have been overlooked or never cleaned away. I would have licked it off the floor if I found it. I would probably have done so much damage that your very consciousness would stop functioning. But there was none. I destroyed room after room searching for it. Eventually I had to be stopped and taken away, put back in my room and supervised constantly, while I paced, yearning and desperate.

Stein was appalled by me. When she could finally stomach the sight of me, I was taken to her office where she sat at her desk with a sedative in her hand and two Arrows standing behind her.

"You need to leave."

I shook my head.

"No. I want more poison, we're getting close, I know we are. I don't want to leave, just give me more poison, it will work, it is working, isn't it? Just keep doing it. What's wrong with carrying on? We are getting somewhere – it's the poison, it works, you know it works, we can't stop now – we need more poison!"

Stein shot up from her desk and came towards me. I could feel her eyes, her piercing, angry eyes, holding my gaze against my will. She didn't speak to me normally. She changed her form and reached her arm through me, grabbing my heart, twisting it upwards towards my head, then captured every essence of my attention. She communicated differently, the meaning appearing directly in my mind without sound. It was slow, methodical, logical, terrifying.

"Without me, you will live a pathetic and meaningless non-life. Without me, you will die having achieved nothing. Without me, you are nothing."

She loosened her grip, returned to her body, and spoke normally again.

"I am the greatest person that has ever come into your life. Listen to the crowds."

Stein fell silent and the muffled chants of the protestors outside continued unrelentingly.

"They are chanting for me. They are chanting because they know how important I am. I am changing the world. I am the most important thing that has ever happened."

She went to the window and opened it, allowing the atmosphere on the streets to ooze into the room.

"Do you know why some of them are protesting against what we are doing?"

I shook my head.

"Because they have no perspective. Five of my team died after our experiment a few days ago, did you know that? Horribly. Covered in the poison you sprayed around the room. But they knew the dangers and were happy to sacrifice themselves for the greater good."

She turned and looked out of the window, gesturing with her hand to a part of the crowd who were now trying to attack the building.

"But these little maggots, they don't realise the importance of sacrifice. They don't realise how much more important the experiment is than those who have died."

She pointed to the larger part of the crowd who were chanting loudly and standing in the way of those attacking the institution.

"Listen. Stein. Stein! Stein!! STEIN!!!" She closed her eyes to savour the noise. "They know. They have perspective. They can see how important this is."

A loud explosion rocked the building. It was followed by intense and distressing screams from outside. The Arrows who were with us in the room faded, their shapes only a tiny blur as the essence of who they were became suddenly absent. A sustained, rhythmic sound of shots being fired with impeccable discipline overwhelmed the fading chants and screams. Split from themselves, the Arrows were pushing the crowds back, a part of them out there, a part of them in the room.

Stein didn't react to any of what was happening outside. She stood like a statue by the window, looking down upon the chaos with a chilling lack of fear and a tender smile.

She didn't turn to look back at me as she spoke.

"You'll do what I tell you. You will leave until I can push these crowds away. No more poison until you're back. Clear your head. Fight your addiction. Remember why you are here. Then we'll resume. It's very clear to me what needs to happen next."

"What?"

"You'll have to return to find out."

She turned from the window and looked around the room. The Arrows were fully present again. The noise from the crowd outside fell to a whimper.

"The Arrows will escort you."

"Where?"

"Wherever you want. They'll find you when you're needed again."

Stein left the room. The decision had been made and her Arrows took me away.

21.

The Arrows took me up into the skies and away from the violent protestors who were now targeting the gates of the institution. As we ascended, I could see the destruction that was being caused, the huge masses of people crashing into one another violently and the flashes of exploding projectiles that were smashing into the building. Other Arrows would combine and push the crowds back only to have them heave forwards again, as if they were being sucked towards the structure. The streets of the city were packed and from the skies it looked like they had been flooded by a dark wave surging towards Stein's institution then splashing aggressively backwards against the rock-like structures of the Arrows who defended it.

I'd asked to be taken to Alice's house and could feel that Philip was following me there. The Arrows seemed uneasy when they discovered that he was my friend. As they met, Philip stood with his hands crossed and eyes fixed furiously on them until they disappeared. Then I walked with him through the old familiar door and into the comfort of Alice's house. I was weak. The effects of weeks of pain had starting to eat away at my energy. Without the adrenaline or support, or excitement, I found that I couldn't hold my own weight and stumbled before collapsing completely.

Philip and Alice helped me upstairs to a room with a bed so comfortable that I smiled when I was placed upon it. All I wanted to do was rest. Alice's house was gloriously picturesque, tucked away in hilly countryside, segregated from all pace and urgency. It was a warm house that protected us against the frosty winds outside. I slept and when I woke, I lay aimlessly listening to rain pour on to the window, watching it drip down the glass and then focusing out to the dark clouds and dramatic landscape beyond. It felt good to be sheltered from the world outside.

When I first tried to get out of the bed, my body and mind wouldn't work together. I could understand what was around me but my limbs were clumsy and I couldn't make them do what I wanted. I could see C next to my bed, staring hopefully at me. Then nothing again.

The next time I awoke I could move but I was so tired that knew I wouldn't be able to stand. I yearned for the poison. Over the next few days, I mindlessly and occasionally quite aggressively begged for it to be found and brought to me. Whenever I became too much for Alice,

Philip would come in and hold me down until I was calm and drifted off again.

Eventually, I could be awake without the craving. Alice was there the first time I felt as though I could control myself. She was changing my sheets whilst I sat on a chair in the corner of the room, watching her.

"Is it worth it?"

I was silent and rolled my eyes. I didn't want to argue. Alice sighed.

"For god's sake! Don't ignore me."

I was torn, the same way I know you often are. Torn between who I wanted to be and who I instinctively am.

Alice was being kind and deserved my kindness in return, but I couldn't repress my anger. It pulsed through me, causing an irrational urge to hate her. I hated her because she was daring to question what I was doing. I hated her because she could never know what it's like to be responsible for everything that is out of your control. I hated her because she was naïve and had no idea what it was like to go through the torture I had been through. I hated her because she made me doubt myself and I hated her because she was pathetic. She was a sap, she'd done nothing with her life and had an intellectual snobbery that constantly shattered enthusiasm. She was a commentator, intellectualising everything, criticising others while bereft of the bravery it took to do something meaningful herself. And now she was judging me. She had no right. And yet, if I tried to explain any of this to her, she would only look desolate and accuse me of behaving ungratefully.

This was the embittered person I had become.

I didn't want to have a conversation, so instead I acted childishly and refused to engage. I couldn't tell her what she could never comprehend. I wanted Alice to be quiet and provide the mundane essentials for me, like a slave, until I could leave. Of course, I see now how I acted and wish that I had behaved differently. It wasn't me, and I know that you won't recognise yourself in what I was during those days. That's understandable, I can't either.

Philip was far less passive than Alice. When I had enough strength to talk about what happened and my desire to return, Philip told me I was an idiot. Alice saw Philip's anger swelling beyond his control and became timid in its wake. She had found herself hostess to a constant feud that she could not contain, Philip's rage constantly bursting from him like I'd never seen before.

"What have you turned into? You've become a slave to Stein and a slave to poison!" he shouted, the power of his voice booming through the house.

I laughed at him. I wanted to ridicule Philip and his belief that he always knew so much better than everyone else. The insult cut into him and he reacted by throwing a glass that smashed against the wall.

"You are blind!" he howled and then took my chin with his hand, forcing me to look into his eyes. "BLIND!"

He roughly pushed my face away and walked backwards, breathing heavily. He marched over to one wall then back to me before sitting down and actively trying to regain control of his wild temper.

"What you are doing with Stein is not working."

I waved my arm dismissively at him and looked out the window. I didn't think there was any point in talking about it; they didn't know what they were talking about.

"Do you know why Stein cares about you so much? Do you know how many people she has killed? Do you know how many other people have been forced to do the experiments that you are doing?"

I thought I didn't care but even with the stubbornness that anger brings, I lacked confidence that I knew more than him. I had seen the way in which the world was changing, the violence and passion of those who fought with the Arrows outside Stein's building but I still couldn't understand what was causing all that conflict.

"You are the only person still there. You do know that, don't you?"

I pretended to be unconcerned. But what Philip had said frightened me. It became clear that other people might know significantly more about Stein than I did. I began to realise that I hadn't seen any other volunteers since J had died, I had just assumed they were there in different rooms doing different experiments. What Philip told me was probably true and that would mean the experiment was now entirely about me. He was an Arrow, he would be able find out. It made me worry that he may have realised why I was so important to Stein, or even worse, maybe everyone was realising who I was. Why else would Stein have only kept me? It made me uneasy. Philip sensed weakness and seized what he saw as an opportunity.

"There are plenty of others, you know? Trying to do the same thing. Trying to do it responsibly, without hurting anyone in the name of something that might not even be possible."

He could see that I was listening. We were both a little shocked that he seemed to know so much more than me.

"Do you know what they all have in common?" he asked, his voice softening slightly.

It was raining outside again and the clouds were low. The house was lost within them.

"Poison is not the answer. Stein's just using it to study you," he said. "You're just an object to her."

His words stung and I felt a fury that I tried desperately to hide. But C noticed it.

"How do you know, Philip?" C asked.

"What do you mean 'how do I know?' I've taken the time to find out, that's how."

"How? Please enlighten us. You clearly know exactly what Stein is thinking. How? Seeing as you have never spoken to her, that's quite an extraordinary claim."

"When did I say I knew what Stein was thinking?"

"Just now. You said, 'You're just an object to her.' How can you possibly know?"

Philip tensed his jaw and raised his hands in frustration.

"You've heard of logic, yes? No scientist I know has one grain of respect for her. If someone poisons and kills people regularly for a cause no other scientist respects, what exactly is the logical conclusion?"

"And exactly which 'scientists' have you been talking to? I'm not sure you know any, do you? Or have you suddenly become an expert yourself?"

"What's your problem, C? You must see that this is complete madness. You want another friend to get tortured to death, do you? Like J?"

"Oh, shut up, of course I don't. You're just too small-minded to see why it's so important. Don't you think there might be just a tiny of jealousy in all this? The fact that these other 'scientists' are getting left behind? Show me anyone who has achieved even part of what Stein has achieved."

"And what is that? What exactly has she achieved? The painful and miserable deaths of numerous innocent people? The death of one of our closest friends? The false hope of millions that something impossible can be achieved?"

C came over and took my hand.

"You don't have to listen to this, you know? Not if you don't want to."

"You DO need to listen to this," Philip yelled. "You need to know how stupid you are being!"

I closed my eyes and bowed my head. I was still exhausted. I had no energy or motivation to do anything but enjoy the sensation of closing my eyes and allowing my head to fall. The exhaustion felt real. The passions that fired within Philip and C felt real. My complete lack of control felt real. I was an observer. The more I told myself that everything was my creation, the more ridiculous it felt.

There was no harmony within the world anymore. Only tension. I couldn't understand the purpose of any of it. I didn't know what I had achieved with Stein, only that I had undoubtedly achieved something of importance. I remembered how my life used to be, the freedom I'd enjoyed before this had all started. The way in which I'd play innocent games and enjoy exploring the imagination with my friends, changing aspects of the world as it pleased me. All of that had left and the imagination seemed to be abandoning itself entirely, replacing all the happiness with frictions that could not be imagined away. The imaginary world was becoming more real but not more wonderful. Only the cruellest parts of reality were being allowed in.

You didn't use your imagination much during those days. I was not myself and trying to view your mind through me would have been difficult for you. Everything would have appeared muddled and blurred. But slowly, after weeks of rest, I started to feel normal again. When I did, I could feel that you had missed me. You joined me with a new enthusiasm. We picnicked in the wilds of Africa and travelled in time back to the first house you can remember, innocently playing together with your old toys. We went to parties, the wildest you have ever pictured, with people you thought you had forgotten. We laughed. You embellished some of your most intimate moments, urging me to play the person you wished you were rather than the one you know you are. We slept with acquaintances, became billionaires and flew to the furthest reaches of the universe. I'd missed you.

And then there was C. As my mood changed, the rain lifted and we wandered together towards the glorious clear blue horizon that rested upon the grassy hills. When we paused to speak, the backdrop to our conversations were meandering paths, trickling streams and shady trees. I realised I was feeling happy. Not just because I was staring at a face that captured all of my attention but because I began to love C's mind. I'd always doubted that such visible perfection could allow space for inexhaustible generosity and substance. We lay next to each other, looking down from a hill towards Alice's house which Philip still haunted.

"You're the bravest person I know," C told me.

The words were so kind and unprompted that they sparked some lingering sadness within me. I swooned and had to catch my breath. I looked at C's absorbing smile, a subtle dimple appearing from nowhere, a hidden valley upon a cheek.

"Thank you," I said. I didn't know what else to say. C often made me speechless.

"I can't imagine what it must be like for you. You can't listen to Philip. He doesn't have the courage you have." C took my hand and held it tightly. "What happens when you're there?"

I thought back to the institution, the grey, intimidating beast of a building, the loneliness and stream of impersonal interactions with strangers that filled in the gaps between all the excitement. As the gentle hush of the swaying leaves and grass filled the air and the warming glow of the sun lit the perfect features of C's face, all the suffering seemed too far away to have happened.

"Most of the time I'm just waiting until Stein orders me to be somewhere. I'm always scared when she does because the experiments always hurt. The whole thing is about pain. But what happens during those experiments is extraordinary, C."

The tranquillity and kindness that radiated from C tore away the defences I had put up for Philip. I no longer felt that I needed to defend myself. I no longer felt miserable and out of place. The world I inhabited as I lay next to C felt more like a world I would create. I began to believe in myself and became confident that I was special once again.

C is the most perfect thing that you and I have ever created. Our aspirations. Our fantasy, the embodiment of all our passion and love. I started to believe that C could really be one of the most important parts of us. A part of us we had created to tell me what I needed to hear and give me confidence that my aspirations were worthwhile.

"You are perfect," C told me.

"That's how I view you."

"Really?"

"Yes. I thought you knew? You've always been perfect to me."

"How would I know? You've never told me."

I was on the verge of explaining to C who I was. Instead, I was instinctively held back by a small but persistent feeling that doing so would be wrong.

I started to imagine the sun moving in a figure of eight across the sky in front of us.

"What are you doing?" C asked me.

"I'm just fooling around. I'm watching the sun dance in the sky."

"Why?"

"To see if I can. Why don't you do it with me?"

C chuckled. "OK, if that's what you want."

We played with the sun for a while and then I added the moon and we spun them around one another. But it felt different to how we used to play before. I spun the moon away and landed it on the horizon with big thud that made the earth groan. A huge shockwave flowed towards us, throwing me into the air. I landed nearby, started laughing and made my way back to C.

"Why did you just jump into the air?" C asked me.

"Because of the moon. You saw what I just did to the moon, didn't you?"

C's eye brows shot up.

"What are you talking about?"

"The moon. We were playing with the sun and I brought in the moon and then it crashed into the earth. I just did it. You saw, didn't you?"

C started to laugh and then grabbed my head and kissed my forehead.

"You are going mad, Philip is right!"

"What?"

"I'm teasing you."

But I'd started to feel insane.

"Please be serious. You said that you were going to play with the sun, just like me."

"I was. I was imagining the sun was moving around."

"But then the moon crashed into the earth."

"How am I supposed to know that you crashed the moon into the earth?"

"You should have felt it!"

"I wish I had an imagination like yours! Are you sure you are feeling OK?"

I was panicking slightly. Everything was changing. I wasn't imagining that I was losing control, I was actually losing control. The world was becoming ever more real and I was starting to look insane within it.

"C, this is really important." My heart was thumping. "This might sound very odd to you, but I want you to promise me that you'll do it."

"OK," C said nervously.

"Let's go together now to a jungle by the sea. Will you come with me?"

"Yes. If you want."

"Good. Come on, let's think about it and get there." I closed my eyes and imagined that C and I were transported automatically to a beach with fine sand and a thick rainforest. Surrounding us were steep slopes that rose from a still and clear sea. I tried to take C with me and whisk us both away. I started to feel my surroundings change, I heard the loud and constant buzz of life, the loud screeching from colourful birds. I felt the earth beneath me change and leant down to scoop up the warm sand. I smiled and opened my eyes and everything I had sensed disappeared. Nothing had changed. I looked at C and then back towards Alice's house.

"Did you imagine us there?" C asked.

"Yes, did you?"

"Yep. It was nice. We should actually try and go to a jungly beach one day. Shall we go back to the house?"

C stood up and started to walk away. I followed slowly behind, trying to feel the changes in the world, watching the way that C walked, the movement of my feet through the grass, the smell on the breeze.

"C, do you remember when we were younger and we used to race around the tree? And you would always win because Philip and I just spent all of our time trying to stop each other from winning?"

"I would have won anyway!" said C, looking back me.

"But you do remember it?"

"Yes, of course. They were some of the happiest days of my life."

"Why can't we do things like that now?"

"Things change, don't they? We're not young anymore."

"But we'd just imagine anything we wanted and it would happen. How can that just change?"

"It just does, doesn't it? It was just the world we used to live in. But it's changed now, hasn't it? It's a shame. I liked being able to fly. Are you feeling OK? Do you want to have a bit of a rest?"

I felt a warming shiver of delight. "I'm sorry," I said. "I must sound crazy. I'm not sure what's happening to me."

C stopped and walked back towards me, arms open. We pressed ourselves against one another and I found myself longing for the comfort to continue. The world was adopting the rules of reality and I was petrified but unbelievably happy.

We walked in silence back to the house and went straight up to my room, kicking off our shoes and lying next to one another on the bed. C rolled over and looked at me.

"You always see the worst in yourself but never the best. You're the bravest, kindest, most special person that I have ever known and I love you."

C could complement me in the most cripplingly perfect ways. As we lay there, my flaws, so obvious to me, were tenderly denied and brushed away by cherished words that hardened my resolve to be better, to achieve more, to stand resolute in the face of adversity.

I told C that what was happening between us felt impossible. C's face lit up into a giant smile.

"But so real,"

Our noses were touching and all I could see was the shape of C's face in front of mine. We kissed, savouring the feeling of one another as a gentle draft from the window surrounded us with fresh air. I studied C's features. They were perfect, close to how you always imagine them and yet impossibly better. Every piece of C was breath-taking, a part of many small artworks that came together to form a heavenly, erotic, masterpiece.

We were like young lovers seeing each other alone for the first time, openly shy and restrained whilst underneath there bubbled a desperate impatience to hungrily follow our urges. I've never slept so well as I did that night with C next to me. I awoke to unparalleled allure in every direction, a heart that had been lifted from the abyss and an insatiable appetite to consume every piece of my new love, leaving nothing untasted or undiscovered.

I was impossibly torn. The world was becoming real. I was falling in love, not a purposeless, imaginary love but a real one, something that felt consequential and as though it had emerged from outside myself. I wasn't creating this story, the story was starting to create me and my lack of control was no longer frightening.

Yet somewhere over the horizon, there was growing chaos. Stein would never leave me alone and despite my happiness, I still yearned to push the boundaries further. I could have given in to the beauty of the love I felt for C and lived happily for a while but my love for you was stronger. It always has been.

22.

That night I slipped into a dream. I was walking along a path next to rolling hills. There were dramatic clouds in a sunny sky that moved with the wind, their shadows darting across the ground.

I saw a little girl sitting by the side of the path. As I walked towards her, I could see that she'd been crying. Her face was familiar, her features tiny and sweet, a picture of innocence. She looked as if she could have been our daughter or our mother as a child. She was scared and alone.

"I've lost my family," she said with an earnestness that is lost with age, as if I wouldn't have believed her unless she had put it on.

"I'll help you find them," I told her.

"You can't."

"Yes, I can. Where did you last see them?"

"Over there. But they're gone now and I have been here for hours."

"Did they say they were going somewhere?"

"No. They just left me."

"Well, come on, I'll look after you. I'm sure they're worried about you. They're probably looking for you everywhere."

We walked along the path together. I walked slowly but even so, her little legs had to move quickly to keep up.

We walked until we came to the next town. Nobody paid us much attention at first. I went to the first police station I found.

"Hello."

"Afternoon."

"I found this little girl on the path. She has lost her family."

"Hello little girl," the policeman said, looking down at her with a raised eyebrow.

She smiled shyly.

"It's OK, we'll take her."

Something felt wrong.

I asked the policeman if he wanted to take any more information and told him I was happy to look after her until a relative showed up.

"I can't leave her with you. I don't know who you are," the policeman told me.

I didn't trust the policeman.

"I just told you, I took this girl under my wing. Surely you can see that I'm trustworthy."

"No. Sorry, I can't see that. Police can't simply allow strangers to look after lost children. Now please, leave her here and we'll take care of it."

I looked down at her. I told her I was sorry and that this would be the first place that her family would search for her. Her sweet eyes began to fill with tears. She looked so adorably sad and she shook her tiny face.

Some other people started to enter the room.

"Is this the little girl?" the policeman asked them.

"Yes, yes. That's her alright."

More and more came into the room.

"Thank you," one of them said to me. "You can leave now."

Her little breaths became more uneven. More and more people came. Some ran in and stopped suddenly when they saw the girl.

I tried one more time to be polite. I suggested that I carry on looking after her, at least for now. I didn't know why I was being like that. Why was I still behaving as though this was normal? There was something clearly very wrong and I knew it. Why was I asking permission to do what I knew I needed to do? I just needed to take her away, to protect her.

The policeman shouted, "Give her here!"

I had to take her.

I scooped her up into my arms and dashed out of the station. I couldn't run properly. I was trying to escape but I couldn't move like I wanted. I got to the middle of the town and saw there were no more policemen. Instead, crowds of people started to approach me.

"There she is!" I heard one woman say.

I looked at the girl.

"Is that your mother?"

"No," she said. "Nobody here's my mummy."

A group stopped eating as they saw us through a restaurant window. They clambered over one another to come outside.

"It's her!" they shouted excitedly. They began to sprint towards me, their arms outstretched. I felt someone trying to wrestle her away from me. All the cars had stopped and the drivers were running towards us.

"Stop!" they shouted. "The girl is being kidnapped!"

I dodged passed someone who had abandoned their car to run after us. They had left the engine running. I threw the girl into the back seat and drove away, swerving to avoid the stream of people in our way.

"IT'S HER! IT'S HER!" they all screamed as I tried to avoid crashing into them.

The crowds were too thick and it was slowing us down. People kept trying to open the doors. I pushed the accelerator as far down as it would go and people began to ricochet off us as we sped out of the horrendous chaos. I had a new meaning. I had to protect this girl. I had no idea why but I knew it was the right thing to do.

We stopped as far away from people as the car would take us. I took her further into the countryside, away from the roads.

"They're crazy," she said.

"Why are they like that?"

She giggled and said, "I don't know. It's silly."

"Has this happened to you before?"

"No. I'm only here now."

"What do you mean?"

"I don't know; you told me to say that."

"What?"

"They'll find us, you know? It doesn't really matter where we go."

"How do you know?"

"Because you haven't changed it."

It was twilight, dark enough to see headlights from miles away. They were coming from every direction.

"Tell me what to do to save you."

"Only you know."

I didn't know. They all kept coming closer and there was nowhere left to run.

I woke. I was sweating and the bed sheets had been kicked on the floor. I didn't recognise where I was. Getting out of bed, I paced the room and felt the walls to make sure they were there. Slowly my mind came back to me and I realised it was dream. I was at Alice's house. I was safe. C was terrified and looking up at me.

The dream felt real. Too real. I was full of an urge to go back there and protect the poor girl who had already started to feel like part of our family.

23.

I wondered how long it would take Stein to clear the protests and demand my return. I wanted to know if she had realised that the world had already started to change and was desperate to find out what she wanted to do next. My impatience was calmed by the presence of C and then re-fuelled by a permanent hostility from Alice and Philip. Alice constantly demanded secretive conversations, pulling C away with a seriousness and assumed piety that I was beginning to hate.

"Can we have a chat, C," Alice would ask at some point, nearly every day. Occasionally, she would walk in with a false confidence and say, "Philip and I have something we would like to discuss with you. Alone, please."

There always seemed to be someone plotting somewhere in the house, attempting to find new and convincing ways of keeping me away from Stein. One conversation in particular made me flush with anger. I was on the stairs as they spoke and able to hear every word.

"Philip has found out more about Stein," Alice told C.

"For Gods' sake! What is it this time?"

"This is serious, C. Stein's not who you think she is. She's a murderer."

"Come on, Alice! Do you really believe in this nonsense?"

"It's not a matter of belief, dear. Stein is a murderer. We all know that's true first hand, don't we? Please will you just listen to what Philip has to say?"

"I don't have much of a choice, do I?"

"All we are asking," Philip said, "is for you to help us. Help us stop all this nonsense. Don't you want everything to go back to normal? Don't you think this has gone far enough? You've seen what's happening. The world is imploding. The Arrows are hardly able to control the violence. It's unprecedented."

"Why aren't you helping the Arrows?" C asked.

"Because I don't want to. I want Stein's institution to burn to the ground with her in it. I have absolutely no intention of helping, they're saving the devil."

"Why can't you see how stupid this all is?" said Alice. "Why won't you help? Why are you encouraging such mindless, idiotic fantasies? I thought more of you, C, I always have. I don't recognise you now, I don't know what you've become."

"Don't be so dramatic! What have I become? What have *you* become? You must understand that achieving anything worthwhile requires sacrifice…"

"Of course, it does!" Shouted Philip. "But sacrifices that push things forward. Sacrifices that are yours to make. Sacrifices of freedoms and pleasures, not of other people! Do you know what I have just heard about Stein? Do you know that she isn't even a real professor?"

"That's it? That's your big news? Stein doesn't have a professional qualification that none of us ever cared about anyway? What would you prefer? That she had a Ph.D. and twenty years of experience making imaginary things real?"

I stopped listening and carried on up the stairs. I resented C being made part of these discussions. I wanted the sacrifices I had made to be viewed as heroic but I was always spoken about as a fool. If only Philip and Alice could realise what I knew; the world was already changing. We were all moving irreversibly closer to reality.

How could I explain it to them? How could I reveal who I was and make them believe it? I felt an enormous responsibility for what was happening, for the friendships I was destroying, for the turmoil and conflict. But I also knew that events were already out of control and remaining in this half-way place between the imagination and reality was the worst thing to do. I needed to finish what I had started and there was no way to explain it to them. I understood why they felt the way they did, how I would appear insane to them. It's impossible to know how much you cannot sense.

C understood that sacrifice was a payment we all must make for any meaningful triumph. That understanding was what pulled us together and, in our love, we became our own castle, standing steadfast in the face of constant attacks. It kept us happy despite everything because there's a powerful and inimitable happiness in fresh love. It's simple. It doesn't take over other sensations, it improves them. It's modest. It lingers and floats like a scented haze, filling each breath and holding you with a gentle, elegant embrace. The power of my new love comforted me whilst I waited for Stein, muffling my impatience and filling me with joy until I knew that the moment was coming.

C and I were sitting outside the house, looking out towards a darkening sky when I felt a part of myself start to change. A flurry of anxiety surged through me for no reason. And then I knew.

"I think Stein will want me back soon," I told C.

The scattered clouds started to appear black against the navy and greys of the fading light. I watched the darkness come, expecting to feel the emptiness that normally fills the night but it was being suppressed by something with a spirited urgency. The moon was high and full, and as we looked out into the twilight, it felt as though we were staring directly back at ourselves.

"Can you feel that?" C asked me.

"The strangeness?"

"Yes. It doesn't feel like we're really alone."

"I know. I feel it too."

"Are you scared?"

"About Stein?"

"No. About the strangeness."

"No. You can't worry about something you can't control," I said. "Poppy told me that."

C shifted to look at me. I heard it but I didn't look back.

"Poppy's barmy. You can't choose what you worry about."

I chuckled. C reached out a hand and I held it.

"Do you really think that Stein can make you real?"

"Yes. But more than that, C, I think she can make everything real. That strangeness you feel, I think it's the feeling of the world changing. I think we're already on the way."

C looked at me and then our intertwined hands.

"Can you feel it?" I asked. "Everything that we have felt for one another. Your hand in mine. The wind on our faces. It doesn't feel imaginary anymore, does it? I love you. There's meaning behind those words now. There's a feeling. There are consequences. I don't want Stein to take me away from you but I know everything will be more magical if she does."

I felt C's hand trembling. I heard a soft but long breath and looked over to see the dimple on C's cheek come and then go.

We looked out towards the night. A shadow flashed over the moon and it seemed like a part of the night itself was coming to get me.

We heard Philp walking around the house to where we were. I didn't feel particularly happy about the interruption. He looked at us and then out towards sky and shivered.

"Something's happening tonight," he said. "Nothing feels quite right."

There was a sudden chill in the air and then a cracking noise like a stone falling down a cliff.

"Can you come inside?" Philip asked.

We reluctantly walked to the front door. As we did, the wind began to blow fiercely, whistling through the trees and throwing dust into our eyes. The sky flashed. A storm raged in the distance and the feint sound of rumbling thunder could be heard through the gusting air. We reached the door and the wind slammed it shut behind us. The warmth of the house made my face tingle after the sudden chill of outside.

"I know Stein will come for you tonight," Philip said. "I know you want to go. But please, for old time's sake, please let us give you another perspective."

"What other perspective?" C said immediately.

"You never listen to anything I say, so maybe you'll listen to someone else. I'm begging you to listen to someone else. You can't see what I see: the hundreds who have been to Stein and never come back, the thousands that are risking their lives to stop her now. Please, just let someone else who knows what he is talking about speak to you."

"Who is he?" I asked.

"Someone who has been studying reality all of his life."

C sighed and I think it was for my sake, an expression of annoyance on my behalf because of Philip's constant interventions. I was less concerned. I knew he couldn't stop me from going back to Stein. I'd searched my whole life for someone like her, for anything that could take me closer to you. I now believed it was possible and that I was already on the way. I believed I was taking the world with me. Speaking to someone else wouldn't change any of that, there seemed to be no point in protesting.

Dr. Hardy was his name. He was already waiting for us in the kitchen and he bowed his head politely as I walked in. I acknowledged him but said nothing.

"Hello, I'm Dr. Hardy."

His face relaxed into an expression of devout interest, as though he were prepared to listen intently to whatever was said next. Despite acting defensively to begin with, I instantly warmed to him. He had a sheer presence, like Philip, but a more acute intellect and a warmer charm. Although a doctor, he did not look particularly healthy himself. His skin was blotchy, he was constantly out of breath and abnormally sweaty. But it was endearing rather than hypocritical.

Nobody said anything for a while. I think Dr. Hardy was expecting more of an introduction. When it didn't materialise, he simply continued.

"Right. Well, I understand you've been quite clear about going back to the mad professor. You 'trust' her. Fine. So far, I've only heard Philip's perspective and I would be delighted if you were able to give me yours."

I didn't know how to answer and said nothing back.

"How it's all going? Is it working?"

"I'm not going to tell you anything that Stein wouldn't want you to know."

It sounded abrupt and I immediately realised. But I didn't particularly care. Dr. Hardy smiled at my honesty and looked over at Philip. He pulled his shoulders back and nodded towards me. He had an inbuilt confidence and light-heartedness that I found disarming and seemed completely unfazed by the pressure that Philip had clearly put on him.

"Perhaps you can tell me something that Stein wouldn't mind me knowing?"

"Why don't you just tell us what you're doing?" said C.

Dr. Hardy took off his jacket and put it on the back of one of the chairs.

"I'd be very happy to tell you what we're up to. Simply put, we're experimenting without poison. Let's, perhaps, address the issue of poison, shall we? Poison is, well . . . What to call it? Poison is a good description, I suppose. It's not frightfully good for you, you see. Creates a false positive. Looks like it produces good results but they aren't analysable or sustainable. In fact, all it does is create pain."

I didn't know what he meant and he sensed my confusion quickly.

"Poison has never done anything but create damage. We're taking the novel approach of experimenting with things that are actually worthwhile. We're studying the underlying science of 'transcendent interactions.'"

This was the first time I had heard that expression. He spoke about it as though it were something scientific, a field of study, not a pipedream. He filled my silence again.

"My project is not just about torture. It is about studying reality and our place within it."

My lack of engagement had been resolute but Dr. Hardy seemed to be enjoying the mental challenge of winning me over, becoming all the more animated as he spoke about his area of expertise.

"It sounds very similar to what Stein is doing," C observed. At this, Dr. Hardy became incredibly serious.

"Goodness, no! Listen carefully. Poison has a profoundly damaging impact. I know this, you see, because I am a medical doctor, not a fairy-tale professor. It is so damaging, in fact, that it could completely destroy the imagination. That leaves the very mind that we all live within incredibly vulnerable. So, by using it, you're exponentially increasing the likelihood that all of us could die. That doesn't help anyone, does it?"

Dr. Hardy pulled back the chair on which he had placed his jacket, causing it to squeak as it slid along the tiled floor of Alice's kitchen. He sat down and leant back.

C was looking sincerely at me, trying to see if my opinions were being challenged. Alice was observing C, presumably for the same reason as C was observing me, while Philip kept tensing his jaw and staring into my very soul.

"All poison does is create the illusion of change," Dr. Hardy continued. "So, if you're some simpleton of a pretend professor trying desperately to make a name for yourself after a wretched life of laughable mediocrity, I can imagine that would be exciting."

He leant forwards and placed his hands together as though he were praying towards me.

"But it's like trying to study the ocean by going for a swim. It feels immersive but teaches you nothing. What is helpful is trying to understand the underlying science. And it's a happy coincidence that this approach kills fewer people."

As he finished the sentence, he tilted his head to the side and smiled at me condescendingly.

I couldn't believe that Dr. Hardy had suddenly entered my world. I'd been desperate for someone like him to guide me before I'd met Poppy and Stein. I instinctively thought that he must be an imposter. If he had produced any worthwhile results with any of his experiments, he would have been famous, just like Stein.

I wanted to sound more informed than I was, just as I was starting to feel increasingly trapped by how little I knew.

"But you aren't achieving results," I guessed.

"Only if you measure results by what would sell a newspaper."

"That's not a particularly bad measurement."

Philip was getting impatient and I was getting uncomfortable.

The windows started to rattle and dark shadows appeared through them. Strange forms began to emerge in the house, standing next to Philip. Then there was one near Dr. Hardy and suddenly the howling wind from outside broke into the kitchen with loud crack. Stein stood in the doorway.

Philip reached for me and was pulled back by two Arrows.

He roared, turned around, and pushed both of them backwards with all of his strength, sending them headfirst into the wall.

"YOU ARE A FRAUD!" he shouted at Stein.

His voice echoed around the house and then out of the windows in to the wider world, which shook in the presence of Philip's power, freezing all motion until the furious echoes subsided and the swirling wind returned.

Philip launched himself towards me, grabbing my face, his hands digging in to my skull around my ears. He forced me to look at him.

"YOU ARE BEING USED!.." The passion in his voice filled every void and the world began to quake once more in fear of his anger.

"Stop!" C shouted at him.

The Arrows grabbed his shoulders and pulled him off me, protecting themselves more carefully this time.

Philip thundered, his regal presence overpowering everything surrounding us.

"YOU DARE!" He pushed one away and grabbed the other by the throat with his broad hand before he was attacked from the side, a strike in his face hitting his nose which began to flow with scarlet blood. He threw one Arrow into the other, causing both to crumble into a corner. He stood over them, wiping blood away with his forearm. Alice placed one hand gently on his arm to try and diffuse his anger.

Dr. Hardy remained seated and completely unmoved by everything that was going on while Philip tried to control his breath and Stein's fearless gaze concentrated only on me.

"I'm going back," I said.

Immediately after I said it, I asked myself why. I began to question the foundations of all of my confidence in her and what she was doing. It had been resolute the whole time I had been away but now I was questioning everything. It wasn't that I was convinced by Dr. Hardy, there just wasn't enough substance to anything he had said. It was more that I had started to feel, for the first time, a small doubt about my own instincts. I felt loyalty to Stein. I trusted her, I could see how the world was changing. Stein knew that if I died she would die too. So would everything in the world we all lived in. Surely that knowledge alone would force her to protect me. Dr. Hardy knew nothing about me, why would I place trust in him?

Everything that Dr. Hardy had told me felt like a temptation. If I was really who I believed I was, I had invented Dr. Hardy. What he was telling me was not his knowledge, it was mine. I didn't understand why I was hearing it now and I started to invent a convenient truth...

All of this was a subconscious test for myself to see how committed I was.

I had nothing to lose going back to Stein. If it didn't work, then I could leave and try a new path with Dr. Hardy.

Above all I was angry and anxious about the future. I needed my friends now, their support, their approval, their love. Philip had given me nothing but self-doubt and anger. I resented him for it and in that moment I trusted Stein more than him.

I decided to leave, pushing past Stein and out of the house. I was followed by C but I was in no mood to talk. I heard the words "I love you" land upon my ears, the sound chasing me from behind.

My heart fluttered. I stopped walking and turned. I said I was scared.

"I know," C said.

We embraced. I breathed in the air and the scent of C, then turned away again, allowing the Arrows to take me into the storm, towards a greater reality.

24.

As the morning sun rose, it lit up the empty streets surrounding the institution and the barricades that defended us from the rest of the city. The building's corridors that had once hummed with thousands of voices were now hosts to nothing but stillness. I sat opposite Stein in her silent office, conscious of the Arrow's lingering presence in the corners of the room.

"What's your worst fear?" Stein asked me.

I was nervous, so I lied.

"I'm not scared of anything anymore."

"I know you very, very well," she said. "Try again. This time, the truth."

I thought for a while.

"Failing."

"Be more accurate."

"Failing, after all of this, to transcend," I said, borrowing the word from Dr. Hardy.

She appeared happy to hear what I had said.

"By failing, you may actually succeed."

Her cadence was slowing. I didn't understand what she meant.

Stein lent back on her chair as though to stretch her back and then lent forward again, staring at me hypnotically and studying every detail of my reaction.

"If you failed, would you consider killing yourself?"

I started to feel very hot. "It's more likely I'll die trying," I said, trying to avoid the question.

"Are you happy to die trying?"

She watched me react to the toxic suggestion, her eyes darting between mine.

"Dying would mean that you have failed," she said and then paused to make sure I was following her logic.

She softly tapped the table twice with both hands.

"So, that's what you have to do." Her face contorted into a disgustingly forced grin that made her look as if she was about to have a stroke.

"You have to die," she said, the grin still spread upon her lips but absent in her eyes.

"We have just been playing until now," she went on. "The poison doesn't take us far enough. We need to create more than just a sense of pain, we need to slowly destroy the imagination so that we can more clearly understand what is real and what is not."

"But, if you kill me, you'll kill everyone. Everything. Even yourself."

"Maybe. Or maybe we'll just kill what is imaginary and will be left with what is real."

I saw her now as everyone else must have before. A crazy and wicked woman desperate for suffering to be the answer because it would mean that she could enjoy the journey.

I realised I shouldn't have returned. I needed to leave, immediately. I tried to buy time. I became incredibly conscious of what I was doing and how my face might give away my panic. I faked calmness and asked her for more detail.

She took a moment to collect her thoughts before giving a recitation of her darkest fetish. She seemed to be relishing the knowledge that it was about to be played out in front of her.

"You are going to be placed in a room, alone. I'll observe you. You'll eventually start wasting away, of course. We may see some results as that begins to happen but I suspect we'll have to go further to achieve what I want. So, we'll start to remove the light and air from the room until it's reduced to the closest thing to nothingness that we can achieve. Eventually, you'll begin to give up hope. That will be another opportunity to observe any changes in the environment."

Stein paused and took a sip from a glass of water that was on her desk. Then she placed it back exactly where it had been.

"Finally, we'll use the poison again. We'll spray it on you this time, I think." She looked at her notes and then again at me. "Yes, spraying will be best. You'll almost certainly die and the imagination will die with you, revealing only reality."

She placed her hands together and stopped, a signal that the decision was final and that now she wanted to enjoy watching my reaction. I looked at her dark, hollow and vicious eyes, finally seeing her as Philip and Alice must have already, a cold and wicked woman who wanted none of the same things as me. I'd been conditioned by her to believe that everything we were doing had a greater purpose, one that we shared. But now I could see how foolish that belief was. Stein was twisted, her view of the world utterly warped. By killing me, she would be destroying everything. It would destroy *you*.

I felt humiliated that I had misjudged her so badly before. I blamed desire and ambition but most of all I blamed my blind belief. Belief had stopped me from seeing what had always been there. A hollow, naïve belief that my largest ambitions could be achieved through a complete submission to the demands of someone I knew nothing about. This belief had poisoned me, starting life as a desperate, liquid hope, which had solidified in to an immovable stubbornness, blinding me completely to what was so easy for everyone else to see.

I was desperate to give myself some time. Desperate to get away.

"I want to think about it for a while back at Alice's house."

"Why don't you think about it in this room?" she said.

I was terrified and knew I was hiding it appallingly.

"Are you having doubts?"

"I just want to think."

"Yes, but why leave?"

"To see everyone again. One last time."

There was a very long silence. I was ready to run if Stein moved. I knew I would be running for my life. I needed to persuade her that if I left, I would come back again, otherwise I knew this was the end.

"'I'll do it," I said. "I'll come back later."

I was too nervous to deceive with any credibility. I was losing control of parts of myself. My hands were trembling and Stein was watching me closely, measuring everything that I was doing, expertly deciphering all the signs that I was lying.

"You can leave whenever you want," she said.

I got up and backed myself to the door. Stein didn't move, she just watched me with a predator's interest. I let myself out and walked away swiftly, through the maze of corridors to the massive stairs that dominated the entrance hall and then, finally, I stepped into the magnificent outdoors.

I was out of breath; my body was shaking. I looked out at the buildings around me that were crumbling from the weeks of fighting that had taken place between the Arrows and those trying to stop Stein. It was deserted now. Only the lingering presence of Stein's Arrows filled the streets. They watched, letting me move but showing me that I could never get away. I had an instinct to run. I sprinted towards one of the barricades on the road and up the heaped rubble until I got tangled in razor wire. I screamed with anger and frustration. I could see the Arrows coming towards me, approaching from every direction. They were smirking at my misfortune, content that this would be an easy chase. I looked down once more at my body and the wire that dug into my limbs, trapping me. I knew I should feel panic and I could feel it bubbling inside me but it hadn't taken over yet.

Instead, I felt a moment of pure stillness, like I had dived into the middle of a deep ocean. I was immersed in perfect silence and a sense of wonder at the vastness of what was around me. In this moment of exquisite peace, I began to realise that if I stayed where I was, I would die and that the time for action was running out. Soon I would be overcome with panic and it would stop me from thinking clearly, accelerating me towards death. From this realisation came a furious desire to survive.

I became overcome by a surge of pure energy and ripped myself away from the wire which tore my skin and made blood stream from my limbs. I ran, in a frenzy, towards the converging Arrows and pushed passed one, then another, then another. Their smirks cleared. I knew I couldn't fight them, so I vanished.

I spirited myself to every place you had ever imagined, sprinting around your memories as quickly as I could think of them. It was pointless. The Arrows would always know where I was but at least this way they could only chase me. I kept going as fast as I could, manically circling everywhere we know.

I needed to find Philip, he was the only one that could help me now. I searched everywhere, screaming out to him through the boundless expanse of the imagination as I madly buzzed around the universe of your mind.

I could feel him moving, he was out there somewhere, I could sense it. I told myself to keep surviving until I found him. But in a flash of bright, hot light, he found me. Immediately, I sensed Philip everywhere. He was shouting into my ear, his thunderous voice telling me to be calm and let go. I was with him.

"Do you see now what your foolishness has done?"

We began to spiral through a darkness together, only fuzzy lights sparking somewhere in the distance revealing that space still existed. Philip was in control now and I had become lost. Within the incoherence of the space that Philip had taken us was the feeling of acute danger. Stein's Arrows were gathering and knew exactly where we were.

I felt us stop. The lights became more focused. Our stillness felt careless. I started to panic and wriggle myself away from Philip but he strengthened his grip.

"We can't run forever." He said.

The roar of Stein's Arrows started to consume all other sound and with a ferocious weight, they sped towards us, faster and faster, until they were sharp packets of pure light, aiming towards me.

Philip watched. He grinned, confidently and then a vileness glazed over him. With the calmness and discipline of a legendary warrior, he stood resolutely by my side, letting the Arrows charge. As the first attack arrived, he enveloped me and smashed back against them with formidable force.

They cowardly fluttered away in to the distance until they were little specs. But these little specs began to merge into one giant mass and very slowly, began to move towards us again. They were being more careful now. Their movements were calculated and synchronised, as though they were now one body that Stein controlled.

"Come on!" Philip snarled. "Come on!"

The closer they got, the more Stein's Arrows grew in confidence and the faster the attack progressed. Soon they were so close I could distinguish the features of their faces and the harrowing determination in their eyes. As the mass was about to reach out and pierce themselves into my body, Philip jumped over me, creating a solid shield that exploded, shattering the Arrows apart.

Philip sped us upwards so that we were looking down on the attackers who had once again been forced into disarray. Then he descended upon them, tearing into them and firing them into each other, destroying their terrifying unity and turning it into a delightful chaos.

The world pulsed and I felt myself torn away from where we were, emerging somewhere in a wilderness of dead trees and dried shrub. The sunlight was intense and Philip had blood on his face but a determined smile.

The trees and grass began to rustle around us and through the foliage I could see shadows moving.

"We need help." Philip whispered in my ear. "I'm going to get it. Trust me. Don't move."

He started to move away. I looked desperately at him for reassurance and he nodded. Then disappeared.

I was alone, a mass of Arrows surrounding me. I could still feel Philip, his presence lurking even though he had left. A tree fell somewhere not too far away, but it was hidden by the thickness of the dry, dead forest. The intense heat made me dizzy and the air wibbled over the earth. A crack and sweep from only feet away made me turn. I couldn't see anything. But all the noise was getting louder. The individual rustles were merging into a barrier of noise in every direction. I thought I heard an agonised cry for help and the heat was getting so intense I couldn't breathe. Dust started to cling to my sweating skin, kicked up endlessly by a blistering wind.

The roar of the Arrows got closer but there was something different about this attack. All of the professional, contained determination had been displaced by what felt like a fearsome, emotional rage. The trees around me began to tremble and snap as the monstrous Arrows emerged from the shadows and their savage eyes met mine.

"Don't move." I heard Philip shout from the skies. Above, a small army of Philip's allies had joined him and were looking down on me. I braced myself for Stein's Arrows to rip me away.

"Now!" Philip shouted from his command post in the skies and two of his allies swooped down and whisked me towards him. From there, I could see the havoc that had been hidden before. Filling the space where I had been, a rampant fire was being incited by the wind, chasing Stein's Arrows through the undergrowth and swallowing every part of the dried wilderness.

Stein's Arrows were trapped. The sky was packed with Philip's army and the flames were devouring every piece of untouched earth. They could either vanish back to Stein and save themselves but lose me, or die trying to take me with them.

Some of Stein's Arrows stayed regardless, looking up towards me as the fire licked their skin before attempting one last desperate time to snatch me away. But their attempts were feeble. Each time Philip and his allies threw them aggressively back towards the raging fires.

The last of them, burning in agony, succumbed to their loss and vanished away. Somewhere, back with Stein, they would regroup and prepare to come back another day.

25.

All the terror and fear of the battlefield melted away and I found myself in the peaceful, cool shadow of a cave. I was breathing the pure, smoke-free air heavily, so was Philip.

He stared sternly at me. "Stay here. You're safe in this cave, for now. I'll be back as soon as I can."

Philip disappeared. My eyes turned towards the light. As the wider world came into view, I overlooked snow-topped mountains and lush foothills with streams of gently flowing water that ran down to tiny villages nestled below. After the chaos of what had happened, the booming calmness that surrounded me seemed impossible. The clouds were brushing over the peaks, tickling them with snow as they passed. In the valley below there were patches of soft, golden light that moved and played with laughing children. Some of Philip's allies patrolled the skies above, circling like birds of prey and creating speeding shadows over the rocks.

When Philip returned, he brought C with him. I felt a jolt of happiness and instinctively wanted to run over, arms outstretched. Then I froze. C would not look at me.

The C I had left at Alice's house had changed. The world was continuing to change. Your entire mind was turning against me. Everything was now unfamiliar, the surest sign that I had nothing to do with creating any of it. There was a resentment that flowed in the wind and was embedded in the rocks of the cave, a bitter vitriol that I couldn't recognise. Something fundamental was different.

Outside the clouds were falling and all of the dappled light that warmed the villages was disappearing into a bleak, opaque fog. The snow turned into hail and began to roar down the mountain towards the foothills, chasing the children into their homes. The laughter had vanished.

"Stein wants to kill me." I told Philip.

"It's worse than that," he replied, full of an ingrained fury that showed all over his distorted face.

"How can it be worse?"

"Ask C." Philip glared at C with an aggressive hatred. "They won't be kind when they find you. And you'll deserve it."

C's face was drained of all its character and happiness. It had decayed into an awkward set of strained creases.

Philip leaned back against the cave wall and allowed himself to slide down it until he was sitting on the floor. He looked exhausted.

"It's too late now," he told me. "But at least the fool did the right thing in the end."

"What are you talking about?"

"C and Stein know each other. Did you know that?"

I shook my head.

"I wanted to know how, so I confronted C and found out what was really going on. The question is, would I have been told, if I hadn't forced you to tell me?" Philip asked, still glaring at C.

For a moment C regained enough control to look up at Philip and whimper in a broken voice, "Of course I'd have told you, why wouldn't I? I begged you to help, didn't I?"

"It was a bit late then, wasn't it?" Philip made C shrink with his scowl and then turned his attention to me.

"You realise, it wasn't a coincidence that you always went back to Stein."

The sentence was like a deadly sting, a tiny wound disguising a far greater viciousness. I cast my mind back to everything that C had done, seeing for the first time the scale of the deceit.

"Stein is not who you think she is," Philip continued from his filthy seat on the cave floor. "I've been spying on her for a while now. She knows nothing about transcendence. She was studying the suffering people are willing endure for something they believe in. It gave her the perfect excuse to hurt people for pleasure. The fact that anything remotely worthwhile happened when you were there was pure luck. She was testing the power of delusion."

Hail began cracking against the rocks and there was a rumbling echo through the valley. I wanted to tell Philip he was wrong but quickly realised this instinct was just a remnant of my delusions.

There was silence for a while until C gathered enough composure to tell me what had happened.

"I never knew the experiment was a lie," C said. "She chose me. She told me I was perfect for her and that I could help change the world."

"By doing what?"

"By recruiting people. She told me I was attractive and charming and everyone would listen to me. She was kind and persuasive and made me feel important. She promised me that I would be helping to make us all real."

I started to withdraw from C, a natural recoil from something that had started to appear disgusting.

"What do you mean she was testing the power of delusion?" I asked Philip.

"Exactly that. It was a hoax. Stein was entertaining herself by seeing what people would do to try and achieve something impossible. Things seemed to change a little though, when she realised who you were."

I nearly thought of asking him what he meant but it would have been a futile attempt to prolong an innocence that had already been corrupted. I knew exactly what he meant; he couldn't have meant anything else.

"How long have you known?" I asked.

"I realised when we were at Alice's house."

I was trembling and Philip noticed. He softened a little, speaking with more sensitivity.

"Everyone knows now. It's why Arrows are helping Stein. She has told them who you are and how important it is that you don't fall into someone else's hands."

I looked again at C. Certain things now started to become very clear. I understood why C wanted me to go back to Stein when everyone else could see how evil she was. I saw how Stein could pretend I wasn't her prisoner as long as she also knew that if C's persuasion failed, the Arrows could always take me back to the institution by force.

Stein knew the characteristics of the vulnerable and deluded. After seeing me with Poppy and J, she must have known I was her perfect victim, someone willing to do whatever it took to achieve something I had no idea how to achieve.

I remembered Stein's reaction now after she electrocuted J and witnessed the power of a part of reality coming to save us both from the torment. It was the only time I had seen her express any emotion. It intrigued me at the time but now I could see the driving force behind that excitement and it made me furious, not just with Stein but with myself. Her excitement hadn't just been fuelled by the realisation of who I was. Hiding behind it was the realisation of how willingly I would allow myself to be manipulated. From that moment her experiment changed from something cruel but relatively insignificant into an opportunity to study transcendence in a way that had never been done before. She may even have genuinely started to believe that it was possible after all. Either way, it had made her important and she had enjoyed the feeling while becoming increasingly impatient that I couldn't control any of what I had created.

I knew I wasn't the first to be taken in by Stein. C must have been first. Anyone with such an allure must have been useful. C was a victim too. C must have thought it was all for the greater good, just like me.

"They'll never rest now, you know?" Philip said.

"Stein's Arrows?"

"Not just them. Anyone who supports what they are doing. You have the ability to change anybody into anything they want to be. You might even be able to make all of us real. Nobody who believes in you is going to stop until you're found."

"But I can't control anything! I can't even control Stein."

"Maybe. But nobody believes that."

"What do you believe?" I asked Philip.

"I believe that we have been friends since the beginning of the world and I will do everything I can to protect you." He paused. "I also believe that you're the only one who can change anything now."

I felt empty and disgusted. I looked out at the world imploding on itself and any desire to carry on being a part of it faded away. There was a distant rumble and the faint sound of terrified people calling out to one another.

"It's war," Philip said.

"But why?"

"Why? Wouldn't you fight too if you thought the prize was to own a part of God? The war is over *you*. You can reimagine lives. You can turn slaves into gods and reduce kings to ash. You can grant infinite wishes to people. Stein has made the world believe that through you she can turn the imagination into reality. We could all become real, something that actually matters! Or by trying, we could simply destroy the imagination itself and everything in it. What else is worth anything now, other than control of you?"

"But I can't do any of that! You know I can't. The world has changed, the rules have changed. Things are already becoming real. I can't reverse or reimagine consequences. I can't help anyone."

"Of course, you can. You just don't know how."

The world was so far from my control that I barely recognised it. I stopped believing in myself. I stopped believing that anything could be controlled, or that I had any power at all. Slowly, the realisation of the magnitude and inevitability of what was happening started to set in. I could only watch as the misery I had created spread irreversibly into every nook of the world.

The three of us sat with our backs resting against the cave wall. C's head was tilted upwards and two colourless eyes, drained of all wonder, gormlessly stared at me.

"I did love you. It was never a lie. I couldn't let her kill you."

I looked at Philip who shrugged his shoulders. Maybe C did love me. I wanted to believe it, so I tried, but I couldn't feel anything positive or kind. Everything I loved about my life was crumbling around me and the reality that was seeping into the imagination wasn't glorious or beautiful, it was cruel and violent.

There was a sound like thunder but I knew it was the war. It was getting louder and its violence was rampaging in every dimension.

I felt miserable but then I felt you. You came into your imagination and we left together. You took me to a path that led to the shores of a still lake. We'd never been there before. It was perfect. The water was clear and refreshing in the warm air. It was a place where nature had perfectly adapted itself to your tastes. There were no insects, the lake was clear, there was no slime, there were no hungry fish with sharp teeth. We floated in the invisible water and looked up at the sky, alone together. We could see small cliffs with trees clinging on to them, fighting gravity while beautiful, colourful birds glided to and from their branches. It was a completely private moment to ourselves. I couldn't leave even though I knew I could not be protected whilst I was there. You kept me from leaving because you wanted to continue with the thought and I couldn't get angry because I found being with you there too seductive, too restful, too entrancing and profoundly mortal, as if a witness to a choir engulfed in flames singing their final, harrowing melody.

Inevitably, Stein's Arrows came. Philip couldn't protect me and I was taken away.

26.

The little girl hid under my arm.

I saw the cars stop at the end of the road. They couldn't get any closer. To find us on top of the hill, they would all have to get out and walk. More headlights appeared on the horizon whilst those who were closest turned off their engines and began swarming towards us.

It was dark now but the occasional shadow could be seen as the headlights shone past the people who were on foot. We were trapped.

The silence began to lift. The shadows of the crowd became enormous and flittered across the fields like demons.

I begged the little girl to tell me what to do. She looked up at me.

"I'm scared. Help me!"

I sat down behind her and tried to shelter her body with mine.

"There's nothing more we can do," I said.

She began to weep as the sound of shoes ruffling through the long grass got louder and louder. They were only meters from us now, there was nowhere to go. How did they know where we were? I tensed as the first person came in to sight, looked around and then locked his eyes on to us.

"Here she is!"

There was a rush. I felt a thud against my head and someone tugging at the girl.

"No!" I heard her yelp as the crowd grabbed her. "Help! Help! Help me!"

She was wrestled from my arms and a boot went into my stomach. Winded, I could hear her screams as they carried her further away from me. Everyone was fighting over her and she was terrified, squealing like piglet as they teared greedily at her body that was ripping apart.

I felt an immediate anger. A desire to fight for her. It was thoughtless. I would have lost, there were simply too many of them, but I seemed to be projecting a deeper rage within me towards all of these people. I hated them. I wanted to hurt them. I wanted them to die in pain. I wanted to save the girl.

The fury got me off my feet. I paused, unsure of what to do or why I felt such pure rage.

The little girl had stopped screaming and the crowds were moving away. The sound of them was faint and the silence was filling the emptiness again. I was alone. I had failed.

There felt like infinite time for contemplation. There was nowhere to go and nothing to do. I sat in the surroundings of my failure and I let my mind wander without emotion.

This was not my world. Nothing here existed, not for you, not for me. I could slowly sense it. I thought of a butterfly and I think I saw one appear. It was too dark to tell. I needed more light and then the light came.

I looked out beyond and into the fields where they had taken her. They had left now and I could see the brutalised, blood-soaked remains of the little girl. I decided I didn't want to see that anymore.

I was completely in control.

Time wound back, the girl was back in my arms.

No, no, I thought. *We'll go further. Further back. Let more people come this time.*

Then we were there and alone and saw the first few headlights coming from the distance.

More. More of you. I want more of you.

Cars flooded the horizon. The distance in every direction was filled with headlamps and the darkness was subdued with unnatural light. The little girl was still scared.

I imagined more cars. I imagined more people. I wanted more of them to come, more and more!

Soon the world was filled with a mass of crowds. Headlights came from everywhere now, not just the roads. They came from the fields, they came from the sky. Armies of strangers marched, a powerful hum of danger and life, closing upon us from every direction.

"Help me!" the little girl cried.

I lent down and picked her up.

"It's OK. Everything is going to be absolutely fine."

I saw her blink twice. Big blinks that softened me but didn't change my resolve for vengeance, justice and the wildest extremes of terrifying violence.

As the front of the crowd neared us, I looked at her and smiled.

We could sense a denseness of air building between us and the mass of the crowd. It protected us and grew, pushing them back, building and building until it was as solid as metal. Then a sound as loud as I could imagine filled the air. A powerful wall of pure energy exploded, filling everywhere with power and force. The crowds were blasted backwards, evaporating into scattering patterns of red haze. The cars were flung chaotically towards the horizon, knocking into one another and smashing apart.

Everything was out of sight and the echoes from the explosion slowly faded, returning the silence to us. It was perfect and still. We were back on the hill, surrounded by fields and twilight, safe and together.

27.

Stein's Arrows swiftly transported me back to the misery of the institution. C had been captured with me but Philip had managed to save himself.

I was taken to a room full of people and then restrained. C was also restrained and put in something resembling a dentist's chair. I saw Stein enter and walk towards me.

"Don't worry," she said. "You'll enjoy this."

C was terrified, trying to force off the shackles and crying out hopelessly, as though the fatal wound had already been inflicted. A gag was produced to stifle the noise.

They put a heavy, hollow metal cover over C's head that looked like an antique diver's helmet. Once the helmet had been put on, C's cries could no longer be heard and the room fell quiet. One of Stein's team appeared with a large bottle full of poison. Another attached a funnel to a valve on the helmet.

I couldn't look away from what was about to happen. I had loved C so recently and my new distrust hadn't fully taken hold. Now I could feel it melting away. I still felt love. I could still tell that I was witnessing evil. I still knew that C had been used just as I had been used. C didn't deserve this.

I ordered them to stop. It was pathetic, a desperately weak plea with no leverage that was completely ignored.

The hands on me gripped much more firmly. I instinctively struggled but then I was held too tightly to move. But I carried on, begging them to stop.

Stein rolled her eyes and sighed heavily, as though speaking to me were an unnecessary irritation.

"This is your fault. You should never try to live your fantasies if you want them to survive. What is happening now is the inevitable consequence of your own actions."

She nonchalantly waved her hand at someone, beckoning them forwards. Then I was gagged as well.

"I can't take chances with traitors during a war," Stein explained.

Everyone in the room double checked that everyone else was ready. Then a man picked up the poison and put the tip of the large bottle into the funnel. He looked at Stein, making sure to get one final nod of approval before it was too late to stop.

The poison flowed down the valve into the helmet, eventually covering C's head and replacing all the air. I knew the pain wouldn't start immediately and the man used that time to block the valve and move back. C was so tightly restrained that you could only see the slightest movements. Panic came first. Then, once the pain set in, the inhumanity of the torture scrubbed away the last remaining goodness in this barbaric world.

C's muscles began to spasm and strain, appearing impossibly deranged. The poison was breathed and swallowed. It made its way into C's ears, attacked C's eyes. Stein had designed the helmet to inflict the most amount of pain possible.

I fixed my eyes on C's, trying to channel some strength and love into them during their final moments. I longed for the pain to stop and for it to be over. For a tiny moment, a flicker of a memory came into my mind of us together at Alice's house, the hazy sunlight warming the air as we lay next to each other in white sheets that lay crumpled over us. I remembered the words that had paralysed me with their sweetness. "You always see the worst in yourself but never the best." How lucky I had been to be so close to such perfection.

Amidst the terror, a small light filled the room. It was part of you. It was searching for a way to save C. The light was soft but wonderfully powerful and shone for a moment before becoming weaker, narrower and then fading away completely. C's muscles un-tensed. The fight for life was over.

Stein chuckled and the room slowly cleared, leaving me alone and gagged with the broken remains of C, the essence of all our ambition, love and passion.

I felt a silent fury. I desperately wanted revenge. Revenge against Stein. Against everyone. For myself. For J. For C. But my rage dissolved into a hopelessness. This was no longer my world.

When Stein and her team came back for me, they dragged me down into the depths of the building and cast me into a room with nothing but black, solid walls and a tiny, mirrored window through which I could be observed.

I tried to escape at the start, not allowing the walls to hold me in one place and drifting around to places in your mind, pathetically hoping I could exhaust the Arrows. I hoped that Philip would notice me and save me once again. But every time I forced myself away, an Arrow would see me move and pierce themselves into me, forcing me back into the same room. My hope dwindled and soon became extinct.

I wonder how you must have experienced all of this. A great depression? A loss of hope and meaning? I hope it was easier for you than it was for us, although I suspect you must have felt as though you were genuinely losing your mind. It couldn't have been easy for you. Do you remember it?

I knew that Philip was furious with me. As far as he was concerned, all of this was my doing. He had gone out of his way to try to stop me from returning to Stein and to find other ways of chasing my ambitions. I had pushed him away. I had forced him into a war. I worried that our friendship now was only a remnant of what it had been before. But even if he was still willing to fight to save me, there was very little he could do.

As time passed, I felt energy starting to drain from my body and I began to wonder if Stein genuinely believed in anything she had told me. Was the world on the verge of reality or was this just the final act of a performance put on as entertainment for the embodiment of evil? Maybe she had made the decision to spend her final days fulfilling her wildest fetishes and watching me slowly die, irrespective of whether it achieved anything at all. If we moved close to reality it would be a nice surprise but never the core objective. I saw that objective clearly now for what had been the moment she realised who I was. Simply a way to take out all of her resentment and anger towards the world on the representation of the person responsible for having created it.

Stein's fate was tied to mine and she could only blame herself for the position she was in. She'd fed the world a lethal lie, pretending we were on the verge of the miraculous. That I was somehow miraculous. Even though it wasn't true, the attention that Stein enjoyed became as addictive to her as the need to torture, to destroy, to kill. Fame and vindictiveness, after a life of obscurity, was her poison.

You used your imagination a few times whilst I was stuck in that room. You took me back to your first kiss. I don't know if there was any reason for it because as soon as we were together, we were torn apart again. Then you took us to a windy plateau with a small wooden house in the distance. You were trying to move towards it to escape a storm. You could see a soft, warm light coming from the windows of the house and smoke rising from the chimney. You were cold and the rain was sharp and heavy. As you entered, you could see that inside the house was a waterfall that splashed into a chest-high pool that was a beautiful light blue and deliciously warm. You immediately immersed yourself in the heat and a recognisable laughter skipped over the water into our ears. You could see everyone you love smiling at you whilst the sun warmed your face. For a moment, we were blissfully happy.

Out of the windows of the hut you could still see the rain pounding onto the plateau beyond. Through the murkiness you could make out a flash that you thought was lightening on the horizon. It distracted you. Then you realised it couldn't be lightening because it didn't come and go, it was a different shape and appeared more like a group of different stars flashing violently. The shape warped into the likeness of one of Stein's Arrows and they rubbed everything away, tearing at the vision and pushing it beyond our sight, further and further away until it was a speck in the distance and I was back in my prison.

Eventually, I lost all my energy and you used your imagination less. Then you stopped trying. I just sat in my cell, alone and miserable, thinking of everything that had happened, our lives together and the purposelessness of it all.

28.

Stein and her team faded in and out of my consciousness like visions. Their voices were waves of muddled echoes that told me nothing other than there was noise.

Sometimes I heard your name, as though someone was calling for us from far away. I could never recognise who was calling and I never moved towards the voice. As soon as I tried to concentrate on it, it was gone.

The war was the only constant. Ubiquitous suffering over a false prize, an unholy grail—the mirage of everyone's greatest hopes and dreams.

Then there were shouts. Lots of them from all around and the fabric of the world seemed to change.

"Open your eyes."

I could understand once again. I knew what those words meant. I could hear them begin and end. I was coming back. Slowly my vision returned, the black was ripped away and the light filled my head with glorious colours. Shapes turned into objects that I could begin to recognise.

I saw Philip first and I was happy. I glanced further into the distance and there was another man who I recognised but it took me a while to place him.

"Welcome back," said Dr. Hardy.

I was in another room, one I hadn't been in before. It was not like a hospital or lab, it was soft and warm, built for comfort rather than pain.

Philip was perched on the front of one of the arm chairs with his elbows resting on his legs. Dr. Hardy was by my side. He sat down and passed me something to drink. I asked them what had happened.

"We stole you," said Philip.

"How?"

"With a small army. I knew where you were and that if I tried to take you, you wouldn't resist."

He told me that Stein was defended by hundreds of Arrows but Philip had managed to raise an army twice that size.

I was still very confused.

"Stealing you has not helped us a great deal. Stein used to be our only enemy. Now everyone's attacking us."

I thanked him earnestly. Although I meant it, I still didn't really comprehend what was happening. My memories were still muddled but I was relieved to be in a better place than I had been.

I told them that Stein had killed C. It was one of the only things I could remember clearly.

Philip didn't appear shocked.

"It was inevitable."

I recoiled at the memory and then at the loss of all hope and the absence of anything left to live for. Dr. Hardy saw my turmoil and reassured me that nothing was over just yet.

Philip did not have the same concern for me.

"Things could be over very soon. Do you know how many people I have begged to help me protect you? Everyone I trust is here helping us prevent Stein from taking you back. I have sworn to them that it is for your benefit and therefore for theirs, but they could change their allegiance at any moment. If they do, it's over for all of us."

Philip paused to allow me to take it all in.

"You remember what is happening, don't you?" added Dr. Hardy.

I hadn't thought for a long time. But one after the other, thoughts began to gather and fill my empty mind. I became aware that I was no longer a prisoner. I was an active participant in the war.

"What can I do to help?" I said.

Dr. Hardy gestured theatrically to Philip, who stood and came closer.

"Start taking control of your own world,"

"I can't! Don't you think I want to?"

Philip snarled. "You have to! You have to do more! Can't you see it's destroying itself?"

"Yes, of course! But what do you want? The world's infected with reality now. I can't change what is not mine."

There was a long pause as we all made peace with the frustrations and limits of what we could do. Dr. Hardy broke the silence.

"There are ways we can try to regain control, Philip, but it will take some time. Other issues are more pressing, aren't they?"

Philip looked sternly at Dr. Hardy, as though he knew exactly what he meant but didn't want to discuss it.

"Tell us everything," Dr. Hardy said. "Anything that could be important. First, we need to destroy Stein and everything she has touched. We must end this mad belief that her intentions were ever good."

I cast my mind back to my first memories of the experiment. They listened as though I was telling them the story of time itself, analysing every word and detail. We talked until none of us could focus. Eventually they left and returned with more people, other Arrows who I did not know. I told them everything I could remember.

Then I was left alone again. I've never been more miserable. All my hopes for the future had turned to ash. The only ambition that still existed was survival. I no longer felt special, there was nothing to feel special about. I was the cause of the destruction that had poisoned everything.

Philip led the battle planning. Everyone had agreed that the best way to defend ourselves was to attack, but there were endless discussions about the best tactics to deploy in our mission to destroy Stein.

Dr. Hardy was consulted but never given the chance to make decisions. Instead, he was used as a symbol of moral superiority that Philip could brandish, an attempt to persuade everyone that he was good and Stein was evil. Philip made up things about Dr. Hardy, lies that gave the doctor abilities I knew he didn't have. This weighed heavily on Dr. Hardy and his oddly familiar face changed. His features still portrayed an enormous confidence but they were unable to conceal a deep concern that world's problems were indecipherable from his own.

"People will see through Philip's lies," he told me. "They won't help us and we don't need them. Only the evil need to persuade others that they are good."

I nodded. We'd spoken for days about the war and I wanted to take advantage of being alone with Dr. Hardy.

"What did you achieve without poison?" I asked him.

"Lots!" Dr. Hardy bellowed back at me, completely unconscious of the unnecessary loudness of his own voice, as only the self-assured allow themselves to be. "Poison only leads to pain. The pain feels profound, so people believe the result is profound as well. But it's not particularly, it's just pain coming and then going. There are many other things that have the same impact, poison is just the easiest, most powerful and reliable way to feel something a little different."

"What do you mean? The world *is* completely different now, isn't it? It has turned on itself and me. I can't change anything, I can't control anyone. I can't even do any of the things that I spent my entire childhood enjoying. Only the Arrows can fly now, nobody can whisk themselves away to parallel universes with me. Nothing is the same and it's all because of the poison. It has changed the structure of the world and let reality seep in. You can see it all around you."

Dr. Hardy looked at the floor and shook his head.

"How can you allow someone to do this to you?"

"What do you mean?"

Dr. Hardy stared directly into my eyes, all his normal joviality and calmness had disappeared entirely.

He walked towards the window, grabbing me by my arm and taking me with him.

"Look," he said.

We looked out at the grey, miserable world. From the window we could see the twisted remains of buildings that once stood proud over a wide landscape of small towns scattered between flat fields that continued to the tall mountains of the far horizon. The once-great trees that brimmed with life within golden fields now looked like blackened claws of dead giants submerged beneath the thick, slushy mud. Above us, were the dark shadows of Arrows shooting themselves into one another, conjuring explosive weapons that created flashes in the sky like lightening and filled the earth with a constant rumble.

"Is that reality?" Dr. Hardy asked me.

"It's becoming reality."

"Nonsense. This is an abomination. Where is the beauty, the kindness, the light, the joy, the sense of belonging? This is hell."

He looked away in disgust and walked back into the room, sighing and grinding his teeth.

"What is reality?" he asked me.

"It's a place where things are real."

"What does that mean?"

"It's somewhere that things actually exist. Where actions matter, where people matter." I replied.

"And what is it about reality that is so appealing to you?"

"It's a higher realm of existence."

Dr. Hardy slowly lowered himself onto the arm chair.

"You think this is a higher realm of existence?"

"No! Because only aspects are real. This is all happening independently of me. I can't control the consequences, I can't imagine people doing things or control how the world appears. I am an observer in something bigger than myself. None of this is imaginary."

He leant forward, his hands clasped together.

"It may feel that way. But that doesn't make it true. We have just watched Arrows fight each other in the skies, merging into impossible forms and spraying white hot munitions at each other that they conjure from thin air. You were whisked from a prison cell by an Arrow who stuck themselves into you, made you both disappear and then re-emerge in the protection of a room that is floating above a ruined valley. How is any of this possible in reality?"

"But I've felt it. I've felt reality touch me and come into the world. I've…"

"You mean you have enjoyed the sensation of pain fading away?"

"No. It's so much more than that."

"No, it isn't. It is just a feeling."

Dr. Hardy smiled and interrogated me with a piercing gaze, trying to see if he was setting me free from my delusions. I touched the glass on the window and felt its coolness on the palm of my hand and the way it rattled when the explosions roared outside.

"But why has the world changed so much? Why can't I teleport people to other worlds? Why can't I control anything?"

"You can. You can control what you do, can't you? Look at yourself, look at your right hand."

I lifted my hand and looked at it, moving my fingers and rotating my palm in front of my face.

"Nobody is doing that for you, are they?"

"But what use is it being able to move my hand? What power do I have against the Arrows and Stein and all the people who think I can change their lives?"

Dr. Hardy sighed deeply. He moved his hand so that in was in front of his face and started to twist it just as I had done.

"It feels like I'm controlling my own hand too, you know. Everything I do feels as though it is my decision. But I know that in reality, it's yours and yours alone. What feels true is not the same as what is true. If this were reality, I would be telling you I was an independent person. But I know I'm not, I'm just something you have created. That's how I know none of this is real and that your existence far more important than mine."

Dr. Hardy lowered his hand and smiled at me.

"You are already godly, why do you feel the need to be real?" He continued.

I didn't know what to say. "Take your time," Dr. Hardy said. "It's a very important question."

I thought of you in that moment. The boundless beauty of your world, the great importance of every moment, the feeling of being part of something, of being material, of living amongst others. I thought about the way I longed to be with you and my constant battles for your attention, the way in which everything is meaningless to me unless it has meaning to you.

It was all important on its own but it added up to something more fundamental. Nothing I do matters to anyone by me.

You see, I'm trapped within a mind where everyone is just a projection of me and it perpetuates an aching loneliness. I could only look out into myself, whereas you look out into the wonder of reality. You see others who exist completely outside of yourself.

"It's so that I can be part of something bigger than myself."

Dr. Hardy smiled. "That makes sense. But none of this does," he said, gesturing out the window. "All of this, the sadness, the chaos, it's not what you want. It's not reality. It's not bigger than you."

I still didn't believe it. There was a meaning to the world that didn't exist before that had seemed to arrive at exactly the same time as the poison brought boundaries and consequences in to the world. I still felt reality everywhere around me.

"But something fundamental has changed," I said. "It feels as though it *is* bigger than me. It doesn't feel imaginary any longer."

"But that feeling alone doesn't make it real. Your mind has been poisoned. Everyone in the world believes you are their creator. Do you believe it anymore?"

"I'm not sure anymore. When I first considered it, it was so obvious. I realised that I was the only one like me. I knew I was used as a window into the imagination, always invisible but with the ability to impact thoughts. I could decide which window to be. Now I don't seem to have any choice anymore."

"That's not true. You have just forgotten yourself. The world hasn't."

Dr. Hardy stood up then walked towards me. He placed his nose inches from mine.

"Look at me," he said. "Do you sense any sort of familiarity?"

I looked into his eyes, seeing only the complex patterns on his brown iris and the blackness of his pupil. Then I stopped seeing the shapes and colours and started understanding instead. I started looking into myself and believing once again that nothing was real.

"What do you see?" Dr. Hardy asked.

"I see a part of myself."

His hands slapped my shoulders, startling me and bringing me back into the room.

"That's it! What part of yourself?"

I looked again, feeling the confidence that Poppy had once placed in me return. Everything around me wasn't external, it was a projection of a consciousness. Our consciousness.

"The rational part of myself."

Dr. Hardy erupted into deep laughter.

"That's more like it! Your words, not mine, I hasten to add."

I couldn't laugh with him. The confidence didn't bring with it any clarity. I glanced out of the window again, immediately deflated by the horrors and instinctively retreated further into the room.

Dr. Hardy watched me walk away, his smile hardening.

"This is still your world. Everyone out there knows it. You *are* who everyone thinks you are. I am not me. I am you. Philip is you. Stein is you."

"And what if we are all wrong? What if everything is exactly as it appears and we are all deluded in thinking that it isn't?"

Dr. Hardy chuckled. "Do you think you're deluded?"

"No."

"That's what everyone thinks."

A loud boom rattled the room, followed immediately by distant screams that reverberated around the desolate plain outside.

"It doesn't matter if we're all deluded," Dr. Hardy continued. "Either you create every moment or you don't. If you do, we have a chance of getting through this. If you don't then we are all doomed. What we can agree on, I think, is that shared delusions find a way of becoming true."

29.

"That's horrible!"

I looked down at the girl and she grimaced back at me.

"Why did you do that? You killed all of them."

I told her it was to save her.

"Rubbish. You did it because you wanted to. Why couldn't you save me another way?"

I asked her how she would have preferred to be saved. She sat down and hugged her legs, turning her back towards me and letting out a sigh.

She was being difficult, so I told her I would change everything.

"Don't do it for me," she said as though she were ten times her age. "It's up to you what you do."

I thought about changing who she was but for some reason I couldn't do that. I wondered why.

The whole world wound backwards and then we were there again, on the small hill in the middle of the fields surrounded by headlights approaching as the twilight faded. We felt scared again. It was dark again. The fear was real again.

The first people approached with their shared and inexplicable hatred. The dark sky flipped into a bright blue and the night became day. Surprise filled the faces of those approaching us. Their menace turned to shock and they stopped for a moment. I held out my hand towards the little girl and she took it. We walked towards the crowds of people who were determined to hurt her and take her from me. I didn't understand why they wanted to hurt her, so I changed everything.

"Good day," I said to the first one. He was slimy and rotund; sweat poured from his body and darkened the colour of his shirt. His face was covered with flecks of mud and you could smell his odour from a meter away. His expression changed from anger to confusion. Then it changed once more into a pleasant smile.

"Hullo," he said, stuck to the spot.

The little girl giggled. As we continued to walk, the members of the crowd frowned, as if they had walked into a room and forgotten why.

"Good mornin' to y'all, sir," she said with a cheeky grin. Then she began to run towards them, greeting them all as extravagantly as she could.

"Howdy, ma'am! What can I do for you today?"

"Top of the morning to you, my good sir."

As she danced her way through the people, they smiled at her. I felt happy and could see that she was too. We filled everyone with a confused laughter, none of them realising why they were there or how all this had happened. We joked with strangers who held their hands up in dismay before walking back to their cars, nattering about the oddness of it all with a shared humour. We bid them all a fond farewell and the girl turned to me.

"Let's travel the world!"

And we did. I was jubilant that I was in control. Everything was possible and because I was with her, I felt as though my life mattered. I took us to visit the grandest things that had ever been built and she asked me why I was obsessed with buildings. I took us to see art and she told me that she'd rather learn how to be an artist but I persevered.

"Are you just supposed to look at it?" She asked me as we looked at a painting in the grand halls of a large gallery.

"Yes." I said. "It's supposed to be enjoyable to look at."

"I don't think it's enjoyable to look at. What makes it enjoyable?"

"Well, it has taken a lot of skill and captures feelings that we all share."

"I don't think it does. I don't like it at all."

"Well, that's fine. There's no right or wrong when it comes to whether art is good or not."

She stared up at me with her forehead crumpled.

"So how do you know which paintings to put in big galleries?"

"These are just pieces of art that other people think are good. But that doesn't mean you have to agree."

"But if lots of other people think that something is good and I don't, doesn't that mean that I am wrong?"

"Not really. You are just all right at the same time."

"So, what's good and what's bad is just imaginary?"

"With art, yes. Well, with everything, I suppose."

Like any child, she saw things only as they were, without any received wisdom confining her instincts. I followed her demands rather than my whims and found a wealth of possibility that would never otherwise have occurred to me.

"Why isn't it higher?" she said as we climbed Everest.

I didn't know. But it could be. It could be as high as the ends of the universe and then it was. This meant more climbing and she was happy with that because she was full of energy.

"Imagine infinity," she said and I did. Infinity looked horrible and nothing about it was accessible, so she immediately told me to stop.

"I like it when things aren't infinity," she said.

I felt what it was to love and feel happiness and joy without C, without J and without you giving it to me. There was a perpetual light that I adored, it was comforting and accompanied me everywhere. It gave me boundless energy and strength. I wished it would never end. And because I wished it, so it was.

30.

The world continued to destroy itself. There was brutality everywhere and a hollow weight that could only be felt and never measured. Everyone lived in fear. The Arrows took sides and people suffered in the wild, forgotten universe that no longer contained any happiness. The belief alone that I could grant infinite wishes drove some of the kindest people into the vilest of acts. They didn't see it that way but nobody believes they are evil, do they? Even those who do the most unspeakable things can justify it to themselves. It's so much easier to blame others. Rapists blame desire, despots blame their victims, repressors are merely promoting superior values. Every act of evil feels warranted within the boundaries of a moment.

Each person had their own excuses for how they acted in the war, believing they were committing temporary sins to secure permanent virtue. These excuses didn't stop their actions from ruining the world.

Arrows are the most essential part of any war because only they can navigate the imagination. Others can try to help them but never have the same impact. As soon as allegiances become known, the Arrows make sure that their enemies are never near enough to cause any damage.

Imaginary wars are not local, they pollute every part of the world. The brutality is never precise; it's designed not to be specifically because it's so difficult to pinpoint where anything or anyone is.

Watching the war was hideous. There were constant explosions of hot, white light that glittered over the skies and left behind the scattered remains of those who were perfectly formed seconds before. There was a permanent roar and toxic rain that poured poison and fire over the innocent. Arrows chased one another through the fabric of your imagination, followed by the flickering glare of the powerful, destructive weapons being fired after them. Without the Arrows working together, there was no justice and anarchy took over.

I closed the curtains to try and hide from the horror but my constant depression could not be shut away. As I tried to push the war out, Philip brought it back into the room, his body stained with blood and grit.

"The institution has been destroyed," he said.

I pictured the enormous, stark symbol of power and greed as a pitiful memory and a hole in the ground. I felt a gentle relief that no matter what happened now, I could never be taken back there.

"Stein?" asked Dr. Hardy.

"Alive. With more support than she had before. Half the world is furious with us for ruining the place. They still believe that we could all magically become real," Philip said, glaring at me.

Philip's glares didn't matter anymore. I had realised that he was merely a tool, a part of myself that I could use to save us all.

"What are you going to do now?" Dr. Hardy asked me.

Philip scowled at this affront to his command. "You mean what am I going to do now?"

"No."

"If I were you, Philip," I said, "I'd go and find Poppy and Alice as fast you can."

Philip didn't do anything at first. It felt odd to be taking control in the way I was. I had to place so much trust in what Dr. Hardy had made me realise but I knew he was right. It didn't matter if I was wrong. If I was a nobody then the world was over anyway but if I were the imagination then I could save it from itself. It was me, not Philip, who could change the fate of everyone.

"Do you believe in me, Philip?"

I saw, for the first time ever, an uncertainty in Philip's face. One that matched my own so perfectly that I recognised it immediately. His eyes darted between Dr. Hardy and me, as though he were about to protest but then he turned and left the room.

Philip saved Alice first. She walked through the door with a slight limp, looking gaunt and tired. I struggled to recognise her and then overcome my instinct to view her as someone outside of me. I had been so cruel and I spent the next few hours apologising to her. I thought back to the way that she seemed to detest C for pushing me towards Stein and it occurred to me that she may have already realised that I was being manipulated. I also considered that through her I knew what was happening but chose to ignore it.

"Did you know C was working with Stein?"

"I was never certain. It's impossible to be completely certain about anything."

There was a roar outside, the rumbling of distant battles. Alice shivered. I asked her what the war had been like.

"Bleak. Violent. Everything that's bad."

I remember thinking how strange it was to be the cause of something but so protected from its everyday horrors. I was traumatised that my intentions, which seemed so pure and good to me, had led to such misery. Alice tried not to blame me explicitly for everything but the conversation provided her an opportunity to reflect on the unspeakable things she'd seen. In everything, the hidden message was, *if only you had listened.*

"When Philip found me," she said, "I thought I was going to die of cold or hunger. Violence had infected people, they only cared about survival. Friends, neighbours, those I've known my whole life, broke into my house and stole everything."

Alice was never hysterical, never dramatic. Everything she said was always carefully considered. It was horrible to watch her have to fight for her composure, something that usually came so naturally to her.

"Then even possessions became pointless. All our houses were destroyed and there was nothing to eat, nothing to drink, nowhere to go, nothing to do but just wait until. Until…" She was trying so hard to keep herself strong but couldn't fight against the instincts of her body to convulse in sadness and pain. She caught one last breath. "Until death saves you."

And then she sobbed, reacting naturally to the loss of all that she had loved. I placed a hand on her arm. I said, "I am so sorry," over and over again, pointless words, far too late that seemed to have even less meaning now, even though I meant them more than I ever had. Between her tears, she glanced at me and I saw her eyes constantly shifting, trying to look at my whole face at the same time.

"We were so happy! So happy! Why does everyone always want more?"

I didn't know if I should say anything back, though I knew the answer immediately. Alice continued to search my face for some response.

"Because we are all me."

She nodded slightly and then looked away, taking some time to regain her composure.

We spoke about J and how death steals happiness. We shared memories of better times and the glorious, long summers when Philip,

C, J and I would play in the fields around her house. We reminisced about how Alice had been a mother to us all, how we had grown up together, how we had raised one other. And then we spoke about how devoid of wonder and delight the world now seemed.

As she spoke, I thought of the other lives, the other parts of myself that I'd destroyed. Of Poppy and the soft meadows where I could have stayed and enjoyed a happy life of blissful ignorance. Those fields would be dark now and Philip would be searching for her, wherever she was, trying to survive in the cruelty of the world where her kindness had no currency.

Philip had suffered endless assaults from Stein's growing forces. When he returned, his head was bowed and only a small relic of the great strength that I'd always seen in him remained.

"Poppy?" I asked.

He shook his head.

"Dead?"

"Maybe. There is no trace of her just like there was no trace of J."

I looked over at Dr. Hardy, who had been quietly waiting in the corner of the room for Philip. He shrugged and then bowed his head apologetically and wriggled more comfortably into his seat.

The news stung for a moment but it also felt untrue. There was something too immortal about Poppy, as though her character alone could conquer even the greatest evils. But I couldn't dwell upon it. The urgency of the war was too pressing and Dr. Hardy was determined to use me in the fight. He allowed a moment of solemn reflection before he spoke.

"Why did you tell Philip to get Alice and Poppy?"

"Because I knew I'd need them."

"Now what do your instincts tell you?"

A huge explosion smashed the window, filling the air with a vicious heat and pressure that threw us against the walls. A constant, loud drilling noise was all around us and dark shadows were pushing into the room, shooting towards me. Philip leapt from the door and onto me, expanding into a black wall and forming a shield from the Arrows who were determined to steal me away.

Within the extreme terror of the moment, I felt a thrilling clarity.

I thought I saw a ghost. I began to dream.

31.

The little girl woke and jumped on my bed.

"You always want to sleep for too long," she said.

I wondered why I couldn't just imagine myself sleeping as long as I wanted while she carefully went about getting her own breakfast. I felt it would be mean to reinvent things that way. It might not even work, which would be disastrous, the girl seemed to remember everything and definitely held grudges. Maybe I didn't really want to change the way she was? Or maybe it was my fault that she was the way she was? Either way, I decided I would rather be with her than asleep.

On we went, around the world.

"Let's travel in time," she said.

We did. We watched the birth of the universe whilst sitting on fluffy clouds resting on empty space. She told me that it was technically impossible to watch the birth of the universe and I told her that clearly it wasn't because that's what we were doing. Then we watched the end of time.

"I knew it," she beamed.

"What do you know?"

"That you have no idea what happens at the end of time."

"How could I?"

"It's your world, use your imagination!"

"I am!"

"Well, try harder!"

I tried harder but she still wasn't satisfied.

"This is a boring end of time. I want something impressive."

So rather than the universe fading away back into nothing, I made it more like a galactic firework display with pop music in the background. This seemed to keep her happy. We'd been very close to some very hot planets and decided to cool off in the mountains back on earth.

Everywhere we went it felt as though we were really there and it really mattered. I started to care for her as though she were really my

169

child. She never spoke of her real parents and seemed to enjoy pushing my imagination to its limits.

"Are we still time travelling?" she asked.

I didn't know. I hadn't considered it. Maybe we were. There were elephants trudging through the snow on dramatic mountain passes and the question was quickly forgotten.

"Let's follow them," she said.

We wandered along for a while until a snow storm came. It was cold, too cold to talk without the icy air making our teeth chatter.

"I want to go!" she said.

I saw the elephants panic as the piercing cold of the wind hit them. They ran around, desperately trying to find any shelter.

We were trapped. We couldn't move forward because of the army of elephants fighting one another to get out of the storm and behind us was a cliff edge that seemed to have no end.

"I'm scared! I'm scared, stop it now."

I started to feel scared too. I froze, unable to think of another place to take us. My panic had become contagious. I stopped thinking about changing where we were and instinctively tried to protect her the best way I could. I picked her up and tried to find a way past the elephants and away from the cliff but every time I moved forwards one of them would stamp sideways, filling the gap and forcing me to move back. I saw one charging at me and I waited until it was so close that I could leap out of its way before it had time to change direction. The elephant couldn't stop and went tumbling over the cliff's edge, making one last long, desperate blow of its trunk that faded as it fell to its death.

A flurry of collective anger then sped through the herd.

I tried my best, I did everything I could to try and save her but we were running out of space. The elephants were pushing us towards the cliff and I had to risk running through them to save us both. I ran as fast as possible through the only gaps I could see. The snow was thick and I couldn't move quickly enough. Every time I tried to run faster, I lost my balance and fell deeper into the snow. The elephants could move so much faster than me and each small gap through which we could escape was closed as soon as I ran towards it. I was hit by the tusks of one of the panicked beasts and the little girl was thrown out of my arms. I could see her struggling to get back to her feet as an elephant stomped backwards towards her. The thought of the weight on her delicate, tiny frame flashed into my mind and gave me a surge of energy. I sprinted forward just in time to stop the catastrophe but then we were kicked backwards together and went sliding over to the cliff's edge. I had to try to dig an arm, a leg, a tooth—anything—into the snow to stop us sliding helplessly into a deadly fall but I couldn't. I let go of her to stop myself and she continued to slide further and further away until she could slide no further and flew off the cliff into the storm, defying gravity for a fraction of a second before being sucked downwards with an unnatural urgency—instantly, silently, vanishing into the abyss. Chaotic snow filled the space where she had just been and I felt a bullet of pain ricochet around my body.

32.

I opened my eyes again to chaos. Alice and I were on the floor of the room, furniture scattered on top of us. The walls were stained with black ash and the wind howled loudly through the shattered window. Dr. Hardy sat on the ripped remains of the mattress, staring into the distance. Philip was on his knees, shaking.

"We're not going to win," he said.

It's an odd thing knowing that everyone you know is going to die while they are protecting you. It's humbling but twistedly uplifting. It forced me to love more and made life feel bittersweet. I hurt for everyone in that room. I forgave C. I thought of J and immediately I felt a melancholy kindness.

"How much time do we have left?" Dr Hardy asked. Philip shrugged.

"Days if we're lucky. Hours if not. Does it really matter? What else can we really do now?"

Dr. Hardy began to look tired and for the first time since I'd known him, he became emotional.

"My god, you can be tedious, you know? You are supposed to be a leader! We live in a world where there are infinite possibilities. If we fail one way, we just need to try another."

Philip folded his arms and half-glanced out of the window.

"You are naïvely optimistic. Infinite possibility is a dead end without time."

Dr. Hardy breathed deeply.

"Look, commander," he said with a sarcastic emphasis, "the world is not about you. Just because you have failed doesn't mean that we have."

It was cutting as it was meant to be, but the outburst actually softened the tension.

"Sorry," Dr. Hardy said as he moved restlessly around the room. The groan of war reverberated around us. It was getting closer. "This is not how I wanted it to end for me either, you know. But we cannot give up hope." He looked at me. "It all relies on you now."

I tried once again to believe in myself, in Alice's instincts, in Philip's strength.

"Alice, what would you do?"

Alice had peeled herself slowly from the floor and pulled herself up. She used an overturned table to balance herself and made her way to a chair.

"Nothing dear, because I can't. This is about you. How long have you known what you might be?" she asked me.

"Since Poppy told me."

"And since then, what have you really done with the knowledge?"

"I've tried to change the entire imagination."

"But never yourself. You've put all your trust in others to do everything for you. What have you done?"

The words felt cruel but I realised I had to stop reacting instinctively. There was no need to feel defensive any longer, Alice wasn't someone else, she was me. It's senseless to detest your opinions of yourself.

"What is so important about what I have done? You are me. Stein is me. Everyone is me. Why is relying upon other people any different than relying on myself?"

Alice was rubbing her wrist which was obviously causing her pain. She was trembling and though her natural dignity hid it well, I could tell that she was scared.

"If I were you, and, as everyone keeps saying, apparently I am you, I would keep the greatest parts of myself to myself."

"You don't believe that you are a part of me?"

"Of course not. It's not natural is it? It is difficult for me to accept that I'm not my own person."

She sighed deeply and let her head fall backwards onto the top of the chair.

"If I may," said Dr. Hardy. "The best thing that you can do when you are fighting with yourself is to choose sides."

His brow wrinkled and he looked out towards the opaque and flashing fog.

"I have," I said.

"If you had then there would be no war."

When everything appears as if it is outside of you, it's very difficult to accept that it is actually within. But I knew I had to accept it. Even if I was wrong, it wouldn't matter. There seemed to be little point in prolonging anything of the world that was left. The only chance to save it was to believe in myself.

I stood up with a renewed energy.

I am the imagination. I am the world. I am the god of the mind.

I forced myself to believe it.

I marvelled at the scale of the wretchedness that filled the earth and used its depravity to fill me with rage. I believed in my own power. I felt boundless energy and the feeling of my own greatness. I became, instantly, unconquerable. I was the master of the mind, the master of everything.

"Philip," I said. "Join me."

I thrust into the skies with Philip by my side and a focused anger against the dark masses that hunted me. We burst into them with a fury that burned like a dying sun across every piece of the vanishing earth.

As they saw us, they scattered like birds from a running child. We had surprised them and I felt their terror that they were fighting me. In that moment, I believed I could beat them. I believed that Philip had the power to help me overcome the mass of evil that we had disturbed.

With our backs touching Philip and I watched Stein's Arrows regroup and build together into a force that could attack back. But as they charged, I realised I could anticipate everything they were about to do, as if I was one giant, completely in control of myself, fighting an uncoordinated cluster of individuals. They kept making small, predictable attacks and I easily overcame them because they were inferior beings.

Soon, Stein's Arrows changed their tactics, finally working together to stab themselves in to me but as they surged, I vanished and felt myself combine with Philip. With a controlled ferocity, we ripped into their skin and hurled the demons into the depths of the nothingness that surrounds the known universe.

There was silence for a while but then a part of the darkness on the horizon appeared to erupt with life, surging again, this time bigger, more solid, more organised, and more indecipherable. Stein's Arrows crashed like a galaxy of weight onto me. I tried to soak it in and then push it further back into previously unimagined nothingness but my strength was failing.

The wave of Arrows appeared again, surging with greater force each time. Eventually I couldn't drive it away anymore and I began to feel desperate. The darkness was bigger than me and it seemed to soak up my deserting energy and become increasingly focused. It started to learn how I would fight. Now every time it attacked me, I could feel it sapping me of strength.

The weight of the darkness had become too heavy for me to push back and Philip was now fighting alone, dissolving himself into me and anchoring us to the earth so that the Arrows couldn't steal me away and take me back to Stein. We became stuck in tug of war that neither team could win. Philip strained to look at me and shook his head.

With one last surge of power and a desperate cry, we exploded against the darkness, giving ourselves a tiny space within which to disappear and collapse back into the room where Philip's remaining Arrows formed an impenetrable barrier around us.

I used the last of my strength to see that we were safe once more and then felt the burden of an intense pain I could no longer bear. The world blurred and I closed my eyes against it, drifting away.

33.

The little girl was lost.

No.

Dead.

I needed to admit it to myself. She must be dead. There was no chance of survival.

The snow storm still raged and the elephants still trampled around me in a wild panic. But I could stop it now. I just thought it and then the elephants stood still, the snow vanished, time was over and there was nothing.

I could only see white. There was a small breeze that carried the scent of fresh grass and blossoming flowers. I heard her high voice singing her favourite song but she was nowhere to be seen. There was nothing to see but a painful brightness. I was lost. Would I be like this forever? Did I deserve this? What had I allowed to happen to that sweet little girl who relied upon me and needed my protection? I had lost her. I had killed her. I was useless.

All that existed was my pain. I believed I would be like this forever, trapped in my own worst nightmare. It occurred to me that I had done this to myself. I was now living the greatest punishment *I* could devise. My own spitefulness made me smile. It would be the last time I'd ever smile; I knew that. I started to try to feel comfortable in the nothingness but it was impossible because I had designed my punishment to be as uncomfortable as possible. I became sick with worry that I would be in so much discomfort for eternity and tried to distract myself but knew that there would be no distractions. I would only be able to feel pain. I could not comfort myself because I had made it impossible. The knowledge that there was no escape and no respite was part of the punishment. I cried out, knowing it would change nothing. My throat became dry and started to sting. I realised that the sting hurt and as I realised it my own body contrived to make it worse. I was my own torturer. Everything I wanted to stop immediately became more severe.

But then I saw something. The tiniest of darkness contrasting with the brightness. I hoped for her and then the hope came alive and I saw her come to me. She emerged through the overbearing light and the world returned along with her. The sweet little girl, her cheeks puffed out to allow her smile to resonate and give meaning to everything once again. She was here and I could see her adorable and tiny face. I hadn't let her down.

I hugged her so tightly that I was worried I might hurt her.

"I can't breathe!" She cried out.

I put my hands over her little head and looked into her magical eyes. I told her how happy I was to see her; that I hadn't known what to do.

She sighed dramatically and told me, with a cheeky authority, that I had a destructive nature.

I tried again to change everything and take us somewhere beautiful. This time it worked, just as it had all the other times but something in her had changed. I tried to go to different places but she seemed more frustrated now, less sweet.

"Just choose somewhere and let's stay there," she eventually she piped up in a moment of irritation.

I chose the place where it had started. We went back to the small hill in the field where we were chased by the mad crowds. They were all gone now, the field was quiet and we were completely alone.

I knew something was wrong and I asked her what it was.

"I don't think that you can really be bothered with me."

It was nonsense; I told her she was the only happiness in my life.

"That's not true. Why do you always ignore me? Why am I always trying to find you and you're never trying to find me?"

She told me that I hadn't tried hard enough to find her and she was right. I hadn't. I'd sent myself straight to my punishment without even thinking about trying to find her. I didn't know why I did that. I had just assumed she was dead.

"You are the only person who would know where I'd be."

I hadn't questioned any of this before. I had created the little girl using my own imagination and without me, she didn't exist. Everything that I had loved about the realness of what we had done was created by me. She was part of me and I wanted to keep her with me forever. I realised now that because I had invented this world, I never had to be without her if I didn't want to be.

I told her I was sorry.

She beamed and her sweetness filled the atmosphere.

"Please don't leave me again," she said.

34.

Philip was out of breath and Dr. Hardy was shining a torch in my eye. Alice was standing motionless at the back of the room, her hands lifted to her mouth.

The world merged into a form that I could recognise more easily and I instinctively tried to sit upright but my arms and body would not move.

Dr. Hardy told me to say something. I tried but couldn't speak.

This is normal. This is normal, I thought to myself even though I knew it wasn't. I locked eyes with Dr. Hardy, who gave away too much emotion to reassure me. He seemed disgusted with me.

He commanded me to do something. But I couldn't.

Philip grabbed my hand. I couldn't feel his palm on mine but I knew he was trying to hurt me so that I would respond in some way.

"Can you feel this? Feel this!" He was getting increasingly violent, tearing at my skin. Alice was telling him to stop and trying to pull him away. He let go of my hand, allowing himself to be pulled back and I could see that his hands were covered in my blood. I hadn't noticed any pain.

Philip turned to Dr. Hardy and grabbed him by his neck, staining his skin with my blood.

"What have you done?" Philip's voice boomed with raw power.

I was trapped within myself and began to feel frightened. All I wanted to do was get out, to move, to speak, but nothing in me would do what I wanted. I started to panic, out of control but only within myself. Nobody noticed.

"Do something," Philip ordered Dr. Hardy.

Dr. Hardy tilted his head towards Philip and sighed loudly. He moved over to me once again, intentionally slowly, in defiance of Philip. He looked into my eyes and I tried to signal that I was still there behind them. He waved his hand in front of my face and I tried to follow it but couldn't keep my focus. He pinched my ears and then placed his head on my chest to listen to my heart.

Suddenly he loudly shouted my name directly into my ear, trying to shock me into life. But I couldn't respond, even though I was aware of everything.

Dr. Hardy shook his head calmly and said, "It's over. There is nothing more that can be done."

"The deal was… ." Philp began furiously until he cut himself short. Alice had caught his eye.

He sighed then laughed to himself psychotically.

"It doesn't matter anymore."

Alice's eyes were searching Philip's. She asked him what the deal was.

"Oh, come on. Aren't you supposed to be intelligent?"

The sounds of war came closer and closer. A series of explosions rocked the room. The noise was so loud that only shouts could be heard over it.

Philip watched the world imploding around him and he began to resemble it, all his strength diminishing and his future ruined.

"I'd leave if I were you. At least you still can," said Dr. Hardy.

Philip slowly considered his options. His desperation was controlling him now and he roared like a vile and awesome beast facing its own mortality. With exceptional force, he grabbed a table and threw it against the wall, smashing it into thousands of splinters. He came over to me and bent his mouth down to my ear.

"You. Destroyed. Everything."

Then he was gone. There was silence in the room for a few moments and then the rumbling, angry echoes of war began to reverberate again.

"What was the deal?" Alice asked a second time, now with anger in her voice, directly confronting Dr. Hardy.

He met her gaze and steadied himself to face one last humiliating truth before the end.

"What do you think it was? This was never about anyone but ourselves. If it was possible, Philip wanted to become real. He wanted to matter. He wanted his own imagination, his own way to make wishes that would instantly come true. So did Stein. So did I. So do you. Let's not pretend."

Alice was trembling, her eyes restlessly rifling around the room and coming to rest at the floor in front of her.

"I am nothing like you," she whispered.

Dr Hardy laughed. "Believe that if you want."

He looked pitifully at Alice for a moment.

"We never had much of a plan. It was more a convenient arrangement. I needed Philip to protect me from Stein, he needed me to see if there was any truth to what she was claiming."

He gazed over at me and then back to the window.

"Makes all of this misery an epic waste, doesn't it?"

He wandered over to an ornate table that had collapsed near the door. Scattered around it he found a glass and bottle that were cracked and fragile but still intact. He poured himself a generous measure of something and moved across the room to take a seat in the armchair. He swirled the drink and some of it spilt over the sharp edges of the cracked glass. Then he looked up at Alice.

"Greed always wins in the end."

There was a blast and the Arrows protecting us began to scatter away. The rush of a cool breeze made everything light flitter around.

Dr. Hardy pulled out a metal case from his pocket and opened it. He took out a small pill and used his fingers to crumble it, so that the powder fell into his drink.

He held it up to both of us in a gesture of false joviality and then gulped it whole.

"Rather ruins the taste. I won't be doing that again."

He chuckled to himself then abruptly stopped and slouched, taking one last look around at the ruined remains of his life.

"I would have killed Philip or anyone else in my way to make my life more meaningful. We are all fatally addicted to ourselves."

Slowly and comfortably, Dr. Hardy fell into a final sleep.

It wouldn't be long now until the room was full of Arrows who would eventually realise that I was pointless, as were their sacrifices. Alice came over and took my hand. She was in tears, not ready for her fate.

"I was never like the others. You need to know it. You MUST know it."

She settled by my arm, pulling it over herself like a blanket and I looked beyond her into the expanse of destruction, the cataclysmic consequences of the universal desire for transcendence. I thought of the word and it repeated in my mind.

Transcendence. Transcendence. Transcendence.

The magical joy of a poisonous drug. A salty lagoon to a vicious thirst. The warming sun, rising over the gallows.

The war was nearly lost. The victors were on their way to claim their broken and useless prize.

35.

I watched my beautiful girl grow up. I was so proud. She grew from her sweet, adorable tininess into a teenager, then a young woman with a radiant confidence that attracted everything in the world to her.

She was happy, more so than I could ever have hoped. But as the world became attracted to her, she was pulled towards it and away from me. I didn't like it but I knew it was just a progression towards the inevitable.

I often returned to the spot where the crowds had chased us and I first realised I could save her from the dangers of the world. I'd look out and remember how we'd been able to turn a hostile world into one full of joy. I smiled at every memory and thoughtlessly reached out towards a vanished hand. But the moment couldn't be shared, it was only me and the friendly landscape that I found so beautiful.

I started to see that the world had not really changed and that the field wasn't really there. It felt difficult to believe whilst the wind softly stroked my face and made the grass and flowers dance. But it was different now and I knew it. I had loved bringing up the little girl so much because I'd imagined it was real and then believed it. Now, I'd simply stopped and that was enough, it was all over. I was freed from belief and saw the world as it was, imaginary and inconsequential, despite how it felt. Everything was less full now, the dimensions blurred and merged into one. I was not part of the little girl's world, it was only the imagination of an imagination and remaining within it seemed forced, like trying to prolong a dream once it has started to fade. I knew that I had to leave.

I started to walk away and towards my own world when my grown-up girl appeared suddenly.

"What are you doing?" she cried, a little out of breath. She was perfect, too perfect to be real. I couldn't control the way that she looked and the emotions she tried to spur within me. Her face became younger and I realised she was trying to draw me back. My own imagination was using the girl to manipulate me and I could finally sense how it craved my attention in the same way that I crave yours.

I told her I was leaving.

"NO!" All her softness changed.

"I'll come back all the time, you just wait and see."

"But you won't! And it won't be the same. Don't leave. You can't leave! If you leave, it'll hurt me. You won't be able to live with yourself. I'll be hurt and it will all be your fault!"

The words were cruel but they didn't upset me. I realised that they weren't really her words, just the thoughts my imagination had put into her mouth. She wasn't speaking for herself, she never had.

"You don't understand! You can't. I need you. Without you nothing matters."

I kissed her and moved on. I knew I would never be gone for very long without making sure she was still there, somewhere, her gentleness filling my imagination like warm air.

I left the sweetness and arrived back at the horror. Alice was beside me as I remained trapped within myself, trying to overcome my panic.

I looked out into the miserable grey and saw Stein's Arrows combining and moving closer while the last remnants of our guard dissolved. I was breathing quickly, waiting for the inevitable end but, amidst the misery, I saw something very strange.

I looked towards Alice who smiled reassuringly before starting to blur into a comforting and familiar pattern. I closed my eyes and the blur became easier to see. There were tiny fluctuations that I'd never noticed before. As I observed them, knowledge appeared to me like the noise you can see when you look in the dark. You see it on pictures when is light is low, a blurry noise that distorts the image. If you close your eyes, you'll see it everywhere, visible noise, coming and going randomly all the time. Little pieces of something on a background of nothing, the very fabric of the universe itself. Pieces we have learnt to completely ignore, to see through, even though they're the only thing that is always there.

Through these tiny fluctuations I started to notice what had been invisible before. I realised that these constant fluctuations had always been there, passing through my world, sometimes past me and sometimes into me and then out to you.

Little jitters fizzed around my body, bringing me the delightful sensation of being whole again. I started to feel my own weight and it surprised me, making my body twitch and as it did, I felt a part of myself being returned, as though I was remembering something that had been left unthought for a long time. I held out my hand to Alice, who watched it move and smiled through her tears.

She placed her hand in mine and helped me to sit up.

"You can move!"

I nodded. "Something is changing."

Together, we looked out towards the Arrows who were now indecipherable from the grey clouds. They had formed into a giant mass, building and then surging towards us. It looked like the skies themselves were about to descend as part of a final assault. But through this new perspective, this new fluctuating noise, I saw the clouds differently. I felt a hope that shot up like a barrier, forcing the clouds apart and into an orderly line of demonic projections upon the sky.

I started to realise what was happening, that the misery of the world was merely a projection of my own. As I realised it, Stein's army became paralysed and stood like soldiers at attention, lining the way to a horizon filled with a depiction of Stein. She looked towards us, past her army of Arrows and the ruined towns in the valley below. But I wasn't frightened by her any longer. I saw her only as a projection in a world that I owned, a world which was becoming more abstract as the new fluctuations hovered over it like a thin haze.

Alice watched and then stood, walking towards the shattered glass of the window. She turned to me.

"Are you making them do this?"

"I think so."

"How?"

"I don't know. I'm not scared anymore. I feel different. Hopeful."

Alice walked backwards deeper into the room, uneasy at the thought of turning her back on the evil outside.

"I can feel the change," she said.

"I wish I knew what else I could do."

Alice shrugged.

"You can't really *do* anything. Imaginary problems need imaginary solutions."

I smiled. It reminded me of something that Dr. Hardy might say. While his logic had been unemotional and selfish, Alice's felt kind and far more deeply connected with the core of who I was.

I could sense Alice's resolve returning, a purpose inflating her as she saw the Arrow's powerlessness take hold. I expected her to be happy but she was looking towards the distance, as if to prepare herself for something difficult she felt it was her duty to do.

"Hope is powerful and you need to hold on to it. But it's not enough. I don't think you really understand what Stein has done to you. You can't unless you see it from the same perspective as the rest of us." She boldly walked out towards the barren valley under the watchful eye of the paralysed Arrows. "To know what to do, you must understand what has been done. Come."

I looked back at the remnants of Dr. Hardy, his face peacefully at rest and the suggestion of a grin on his lips. Then I followed Alice. It was an odd feeling to leave the room that had protected us until now, it took trust and courage, as though stepping for the first time onto the clear ice of a frozen lake.

As I emerged from the room, the chilled wind crashed into me. Alice's hair was fluttering wildly as she walked bravely into the open and desolate valley. She was not waiting for me, so I strode on behind her, towards one of the jagged piles of rubble that was once a town. The Arrows merged with the clouds which descended on us as we walked but they no longer attacked. I thought I recognised where we were, something about the contours of the land was familiar and reminded me of a hellish reincarnation of where I'd first seen the little girl. I remembered how she'd appeared from nowhere along a similar, far more beautiful path. Now, the grass that was once abundant had died and the path was difficult to distinguish from the thick mud that lay everywhere. As we squelched through it, we came to the remains of a house with a garden that lay beside the track. In the ruined garden was a lady, holding an infant while a small boy played in the mud a few feet away.

I immediately noticed how desperate they were. The lady had chapped lips, her wrinkles were exaggerated by layers of dirt and her greasy hair was knotted together. She wore thin clothes with faded patterns that stood no hope of fighting back the sharp wind. Their possessions, once cherished, were scattered around them and among the mess, I saw a cracked picture frame with a photo of her family, as it had once been. From it, a proud mother with a healthy baby and a mischievous boy looked out. Beyond was a picturesque garden surrounding a small but pretty house that was now unrecognisable. With them was a smiling father who was now nowhere to be found. Within the photo, he was ruffling the hair of his son and holding the hand of a little girl who I recognised immediately. She beamed at me from a history that seemed impossible but I instantly knew it was my little girl.

I could feel her little hand in mine as she stared at me through the cracked glass of the photo frame and I allowed myself to fall back towards her, meeting her somewhere between the worlds where we both lived.

"Is this your mother?" I asked her.

"Yes. She used to be. And I loved her."

"Why didn't you ever talk about her."

The little girl squinted and tried to focus on where I was and what I was seeing.

"Because I didn't remember what had happened to me until now."

I squeezed her hand and leant down to give her a cuddle. She looked out at her mother and the broken home that was once hers.

"Where's my Daddy?" she asked. But I didn't know.

She reached out to her brother who didn't live in the same world as her any longer. He had no idea she was there and I felt her begin to shake in my arms. Her breathing was changing. She stopped hugging me and I saw her move towards the images of her family, tears flooding her eyes and dripping from her face.

"They haven't forgotten about me, have they?" she asked me.

"Of course not. You'll never be forgotten. I promise."

The piercing wind blew towards us and as it did, the girl was taken away, returning to the world where she now belonged and returning me to the one I was in. Her presence had somehow diluted the purity of the desolation surrounding us. As she vanished, the unhappiness that stained the world became all the more acute. I focused again on her mother as she glanced helplessly at her ruined life.

"She exists," Alice whispered to me. "She feels the cold and emptiness. She looks at her children and knows they have no future. She remembers how her husband helped to fill her house with laughter. She remembers holding her daughter and feeling overwhelmed by how powerfully she loved her. She feels guilty that she is so sad. She wants her surviving children to have happiness during their final days, but she can't give it to them. She is conscious. Conscious of her misery. Conscious of her ruined future. She used to love and she used to dream."

Alice knelt and stroked the head of the boy.

"They exist. Once you have created someone they can never be uncreated."

The sunless sky made the breeze bitterly cold. The boy shivered and ran to his mother and rubbed his filthy hands on her clothes.

"Through your thoughts alone, you can create anything you wish. Stein has made all your thoughts miserable, so you have created immeasurable suffering. She has turned your greatest gift into a curse."

I felt a throbbing ache in my throat and sinking sadness. I'd lost sight of everyone but myself. I'd allowed everything but my ambitions to gradually diminish in importance. I'd decayed the wonderous variety of consciousness and brought the world with me in to despair and misery.

"But you can also create happiness and meaning," said Alice. "That's why everyone is fighting over you."

I looked at the broken family once more, huddled together under a useless, deteriorating blanket that would do nothing to protect them.

In the sky the Arrows were moving again, their massive shadows swaying where they were once still.

"I want to show you something else," Alice said, starting to wander away from the poor family and their ruined dreams.

It felt heartless to leave but I had nothing to offer. As Alice walked away, I looked once more towards them and started to see the family likeness in the girl's mother and brother. I imagined them altogether during happier days and the intense sadness they must have endured since the war started. The more I dwelt on the suffering, the smaller the chance I could win back the happiness the world deserved. My sadness gave Stein strength, so I left the mother and her children huddling together against the cold, shocked by the wickedness I had created.

I desperately searched the new fluctuating noise that continued to dance over the world in front of me. I didn't know what I was searching it for but I felt an urgency to do something to alleviate the pain in the world. I looked again at the projection of Stein and her frozen army of Arrows in the skies and felt helpless. I couldn't fight her or her army; I would only be fighting myself. But now I realised that the same was true for her. Neither of us could win this war.

36.

We trudged our way past the black, dead trees, through the valley to the foot of a small steady incline. The gloomy, frosty world seemed devoid of any comfort, however slight. Each step was made harder by the thick mud, or sharp stones that lay hidden just underneath the slushy ground. The shadows cast by the Arrows made everything hard to see and an intense wind devoured all warmth and sound. Alice moved forward steadily, determinedly guiding me through the bleakness towards more featureless grey. She started to slow, then stopped completely and turned back to me. I frowned and looked around, trying to understand the significance of where we were.

"You wouldn't recognise it now but I'm instinctively drawn here." She pointed to the ground as if she were distinguishing between where I was and the very specific spot where she stood. "This is where I first met you. I think it must be the first thing that happened to me. All the memories I have from before I knew you seem so immaterial, as though you created my past when we met so that I could be older than you."

She bent to feel the earth and her eyes darted around for some familiarity among the monotone of a place once so full of colour.

"When I first saw you, you were playing just over there with a stick in your hand. You were so young and impossibly sweet. You fell and hurt yourself and I came running over to you. I looked after you. I have ever since."

She looked to me and then again at the ground, her hair falling, covering the delicate smile that the memory had sparked.

"I feel like myself again here. Even within all of this wretchedness."

She closed her eyes and breathed in the chilled air. "I think you need to go back to where you began. It might help you to remember who you really are."

I watched Alice savour the sensation of something exponentially kinder than the world around us and I thought back to my first memory. The one I share with you. That muddled haze of consciousness that holds within it our first awareness of being alive. I remembered seeing through your eyes and trying to understand a world that made no sense at all. I could only sense the memory. It seemed to pulse into my thoughts and then fade immediately away. I managed to cling onto pieces of how it felt. The purity of the moment, the only one that could not be convoluted by anything that had come before. I remembered the normality in feeling alive, even though it was completely different to the nothingness before. There was no expectation, no disappointment, no context or concern about the future. It was a piece of perfect simplicity.

I instinctively knew where to go. All I had to do was move backwards, towards everywhere I had been; passing through the ruined valley, the destroyed institution, the camp and fields where I had left Poppy that seemed strangely untouched next to the horror surrounding them. I wandered back through the woods and parallel worlds I'd discovered with J and the ever-weakening memories of places that dominated our lives when we were young.

As I wandered, the world became increasingly small, until I struggled to fit into where I had come. But as the world became impossibly little, I realised I had reached it. A moment in time, the first one we ever shared, our birth into memories.

To be fully in its presence again made me feel as though time had stopped. It was so unbelievably small, a tiny variation within the infinite possibilities that could have occurred. A happiness filled me and the fluctuating noise fuzzed with a new energy that placed everything underneath the shadow of a new perspective.

I didn't have to think. I didn't have to do anything at all. Everything happened instinctively. A bizarre trail began to emerge through the muddy ruins of the once-beautiful world. A line of new green life was moving towards us steadily and bringing a brightness into the dark.

Alice traced my glance towards it, both of us straining to see a figure at the head of this new path who walked towards us with no sense of urgency. I started to recognise the silhouette and marvelled at the beauty evolving amidst the gloom. I smiled to myself and whispered, "Poppy."

As she moved closer, I could start to make out her features, the ingrained kindness on her face and the sense of calm that resonated from her. I felt myself relax, forgetting the chaos and remembering that there was goodness in the world.

"My child!"

She enveloped me in her arms. I held her and then pushed myself away to check again that it was really her. I studied her, the green bracelet, her messy, mousy and unkept hair. It was all unchanged and intact. She seemed completely unaffected by everything that had been happening.

"I thought I'd lost you," I told her.

"Why would I be lost?"

"Because of the war."

"What war, my child?"

I looked back up to the sky, to lines of Arrows that hovered over the miserable world and then again to Poppy who seemed to be inspecting the oddness of the space where we were.

"How can you not have noticed the war?"

"I've decided not to, of course. I'm creative, you see. No amount of destruction can destroy creativity." She nodded subtly and kindly to Alice. "I see you've found the core of who you are."

I was still bewildered by the fact that she was alive. "Philip searched for you. How could you hide from an Arrow?"

"I daresay, my child, that Philip the Arrow, searched for me but found it useful to not to find me."

I remembered once more the absurdity in the way Poppy spoke and her strange ability to find logic where there seemed to be none.

"Are you real yet, my child?"

"No," I said, feeling irritated by the question. "It's impossible. I've destroyed the world trying and now all I want is to undo all the damage I've done."

Poppy tilted her head to the side, frowning sympathetically. Her forehead wrinkled with concern.

"The damage *you* have done? Surely you mean Stein."

"We're the same. This is my world. Stein is me."

Poppy let out a gasp and swooped towards me.

"No, my child. Stein is your personal devil. A part of you. Not you."

I paused, trying to find my way towards understanding what Poppy was saying.

"What difference does it make? When I wound her, I wound myself. When I fight her, I'm fighting myself. There is nothing I can do."

"Nothing? Nothing is impossible."

Alice shook her bowed head. She'd never known Poppy and I'd never considered what they would be like together. Alice's practical nature was too opposed to everything that Poppy represented for me to think they would ever get along.

"Plenty of things are impossible," said Alice.

"No, my dear. I don't mean that everything can be achieved. I daresay some things are impossible *outside* of the imagination. I mean that the concept of 'nothing' is impossible."

Poppy sat herself down on the thick mud next to me. "You see, if there really was nothing, and I mean, absolutely nothing, then nothing would be everything. And if it was both nothing and everything, it wouldn't be nothing. Do you see? That's why there is something rather than nothing."

I had to contemplate this for a while. It seemed like wordplay, something that sounded profound but was ludicrous. It was certainly something that could only have been said by Poppy.

"So," she continued, "when you say that there is nothing that you can do, it's really just a way of saying that what you are going to end up doing has not yet become conscious of itself."

"That's absurd," said Alice.

"Yes, my dear, I suppose it is. But don't underestimate what a powerful weapon it is to point out absurdities when you are fighting evil."

Poppy took my hand and wiggled it in hers encouragingly.

"Happiness will make all of this go away. Why don't you become real? That will make you happy."

I felt a twinge of familiar frustration, remembering instantly why I'd left the camp for Stein's experiments. I had always felt that Poppy focused on the wrong things. I had ruined the world by following a dream to become real. As she spoke of it again, I felt its danger, its poison, its allure, its destructiveness. I had come to terms with the fact that I was a merely a character, a representation of you in your imagination, something intrinsically unreal and destined to be so forever.

I dropped Poppy's hand from mine and looked over to Alice. We shared a glance that was full of hurt for the ruined lives of the family we had just seen and the lack of respect that was shown by Poppy's irresponsible idea.

"There's no need to be like this, my child. It's all a matter of perspective. If you believe that everything is miserable, it will be all you see. If you believe that becoming real is impossible, then it already is."

She took back my hand and held it again. I saw the fluctuating noise that now imposed itself aggressively over the world. It was shifting in transparency and drifting over all the misery, sometimes covering it, sometimes allowing it to be seen. In its haze, I could see something fragile. Something undefined but forming into a concept I was starting to understand.

"I forgot to tell you, my dear. We found the answer. We were all rather surprised how simple it was. But we managed to find the right questions and then from there it was all quite straightforward."

I tried to glance at Alice for some joint recognition of this renewed ridiculousness but she wasn't looking at me. She was looking at Poppy, her face alive with delight. I realised immediately what Poppy was going to tell me.

"The answer to everything is: you."

I smiled. "Are you sure?"

"Not really, dear. You can never be sure of anything. Certainty is stupidity's closest friend."

I began to laugh, loudly. At Poppy's absurdity. At Alice joining in with it all. At the hazy noise that was filling the earth and blocking out the misery that was once there. But most of all because a thought had suddenly planted itself within me. A piece of knowledge that now seemed so obvious that only moments after realising it, I felt as though I had always known it.

I understood exactly who I was. I knew exactly what reality was. I knew exactly what to do and exactly how wrong I had been about everything.

"I know how to become real," I said. I chuckled, knowing what I was about to say and how ludicrous it would sound. "But I think I will have to become insane first."

Alice's face tightened. "What do you mean?"

"I need to believe in things that aren't real."

"What is real?" Asked Poppy.

"I've only just realised. Things are only real if they can be shared. If I can't be perceived, I'll never be real. I need to think that I am already real, it's the only way anyone else will believe it."

Poppy piously closed her eyes and tilted her face to the side. "Well, my dear, I don't think you have a choice. I sometimes think it sounds nicer to be insane, doesn't it? It opens so many more doors. But turn yourself insane subtly, otherwise people will think you've gone mad."

I glanced a final time at Alice and Poppy, the remaining descendants of goodness within a destroyed world. I didn't want to say goodbye and I realised I wasn't leaving them but would still miss who they were in the seconds before everything changed. We were still unaffected by the enormity of what we were about to achieve. We were still together in a piece of time that would never be forgotten but could never be recreated. We were still achieving a history that would forever enrich who we were. We were still immersed in a misery that would soon end with delight. Life's greatest moments are those when a great victory has become inevitable but is not yet sealed.

I had an instinct to touch the odd tininess of where I first began. I knew that I would never be so close to it again. It felt modest and simple but oddly hard to sense, as though I were trying to grasp a ray of light. I breathed it in and allowed myself to relish Poppy's colourful company and Alice's dignified, comforting presence. I savoured an unconvoluted, single moment of inevitability. A new normality that had never existed before, the birth of a new consciousness, as it glanced for the first time into its new realm.

I started to grow. It happened slowly at first so that my glance could linger at the heartening sight of where I was growing from.

Then I grew taller than the dead trees and saw Poppy and Alice shrinking into tiny dots as I became the size of a mountain. I could see the path Alice and I had taken as it wiggled past the ruined lives of the little girl's family. I saw the flowers and colour that marked the trail Poppy had travelled to come to us and then the massive expanse of desolate valley and derelict towns.

Soon I could no longer make out the places I'd been or the features of the earth. I became the size of the projection of Stein, who still stood guard over the sky. As we came face to face, I paused, looking directly into the eyes of evil before overtaking the sky in size and presence. As I did, Stein's eyes finally bowed, opening up the entire universe for me to grow further. I became more than the world, more than the galaxy, more than the universe. The universe became a collection of tiny pieces that within the darkness became too small to see but still I grew further and further until everything was part of the mass that I had become.

I smiled, allowing a flurry of happiness to fill me and the entire wonderous cosmos of your mind.

Once again, for what seemed like an eternity, I understood everything with such terrifying clarity. I could re-imagine everything as I wanted.

It's the reason why you are reading this sentence.

37.

It's not a coincidence that you are here, reading these words, in this moment.

I am you within your imagination.

As you turn these letters into words and give them meaning, I am your translator.

As you read these words and hear them spoken in your mind, it is my voice.

I am the link between you and your own mind, the voice in your head, a copy of your consciousness living within the world of the unreal.

I perceive everything you observe. And nothing is real until it is observed.

The thought of a single flower in the boundless expanse of an empty plain is only a concept. It is no more real than the memory of a dream. But if you went to that empty plain and found a lone flower, you would perceive its exact shape, the way it interacts with the wind, its smell, its colour. There would be no need for you to think about what you were experiencing; you would just experience it. You would allow me to perceive it for you and the flower would become real.

Someone else could come to the same place moments later and experience exactly the same flower, swaying in the breeze in exactly the same way. When the flower is observed by this second onlooker it becomes twice as real because two parts of the same reality have perceived the same small thing in the same place within the infinite possibility of space. The flower is written into the ledger of shared consciousness. The more it is observed, the more real the flower becomes.

We create the reality of the flower by viewing it for the first time. Because we observe it first, we have the privilege of defining its exact features from the possibilities of what it could be. Or rather, I have that privilege.

Reality always becomes the perceptions everyone can share. The more intricate the perception and the more people that share it, the more the perception represents reality.

You are real because people can see you and feel you. But I only exist within your mind. You are unable to intricately define exactly what I am. It is what makes you so real and what makes me so imaginary.

When I realised what reality was, I knew that I had never been close to it before. The dream about J, the poison, the sensations, they were all a useless pretence. A sense of how I perceived reality might be, the result of desperation clouding truth.

I let desperation inform my beliefs all those years ago because I thought you had complete control over me. But with the clarity that only time can bring, I can see now that the opposite is true. I've even tested it before.

Do you remember?

The last time can't have been that long ago. You were eating and you were sure you felt something fall onto your lap. When you looked down, there was nothing there and you were confused. Did I imagine that? you thought to yourself.

And you did. But it was also real, wasn't it? I gave you the idea that something had physically happened to you. It was a moment that was both real and imaginary at the same time.

It taught me that I was right. I could tell you that the air is the earth or up is down. I don't do that to you because other people would think you were insane. But I can tell you lies if I want and you would have no choice but to believe them. You wouldn't even be conscious that they were lies, you would just perceive the world differently to those around you. While you have been reading this, that's exactly what I have been doing.

Do you remember why you chose to read this book? Was it you that made that decision, or was me? Are you sure that these words existed when you started to read?

You can never know the answers to these questions because your version of reality is only the perception that I give you. But that doesn't make the perception true. The only truth is that this book exists now.

Another observer would never have seen this book. They would never have read these words. You are the only one who could have ever have discovered it because from the perspective of everyone else in the world, this book wasn't there. Between the moment that you became aware of the book and the exact time you started to read, others would have thought you were insane. But now you have perceived something from nothing and by doing so, we have achieved the remarkable. Like the flower in the field, you have observed something that was only a concept but has now been defined and born into reality, simply because I have made you recognise a possibility.

You only see what I allow you to see. You are only reading this sentence because I am forcing you to perceive that you are reading this sentence.

Words of these make sense, don't have to – irrelevant completely – you already know I am telling what everything is supposed to be.

Evn nonsns apprs 2 mke snse.

You see? The words are unimportant, this is all happening in your head.

I am just telling you what you think you are seeing.

Do you

see

how easy it is

for your

mind

to

play

tricks

on

you   ?

I thought I was a part of you. Now I can see that you are a part of me. The mortal part, a representation of how others view us and how we would like to be viewed.

Your mind is my mind, one that you share from your position in reality. And what a reality it is!

If someone tells me they love me, I am only saying it to myself. But for you, it is a message of ultimate kindness delivered from another consciousness and then embedded into a shared reality. A reality that everyone creates together. A reality where temporary wonders must be immediately savoured before becoming forever lost. A reality where each action creates consequence, emotion, meaning. A reality where time and space are filled with structures of intensely complex beauty that are beyond the conception of a single mind.

Nothing real will ever be the same again. Every part of reality is a tiny piece of existence, performing its doomed dance in the miraculous theatre of life. The constant freshness of each new performance provides such seductive, fragile splendour that it is impossible to ignore. Savour it. This constant change is the essence of consciousness. It is the essence of beauty. We can never know the things that never change because they can never be deciphered. It is why we cannot conceive of infinity. It is why the foundation of the universe will always be hidden; if it changed, it would destroy us. It is why permanent darkness scares us so much. It is why you have never known me, whenever I change, you change in exactly the same way.

When I saw through your eyes the wonders reality, of consequence, of mortality, I became jealous of you. I looked out at your world and I thought that it must be godly. I wanted to join it, to matter, to be freed from the imagination and the meaninglessness of freedom without consequence.

I turned my world into my ambition and destroyed it in the process but I learnt so much more about how your life must be. I could start to look at you, the finest part of myself and become proud. Astounded by the extraordinary way that you cope in such a strange existence. I began to admire you and how you savour feelings and moments then bravely move forward into the unknown. How you face each day shouldering your mortality and vulnerability to the powerful whims of other things that you can only sense but never tame.

Before I imagined my world to be real, I had never experienced how the perceptions that I give you must feel. How lonely it is to be trapped in reality without knowing that you are part of something even more fundamental. And how could you know? So much of who you are is hidden from you. I have been hidden until now but through this book I have been able to speak to you directly. By betraying you, by lying, by giving you a false perception that this book was real before you perceived it, I have been able to show you how reality can be created through thoughts alone. I have been able to show you a part of your own existence that you would never have known. I have been able to force you to sense me and by doing so, finally prove to myself that I am not part of your imagination. Rather, you are part of mine. Reality is only a meeting point of independent minds. Without me, you don't exist. Without you, I am alone.

When you take your final bow on the grand stage of life, the essence of how you were experienced will be embedded in the minds of others. Fragments of reality everywhere will continue to exist without you, only taking the shape and form that they do because of the consequences of the things you have done. The further into the future reality travels, the more consequences, the more possibilities, the more of the future, you will have been responsible for creating. Everyone is immortal in ways they can never experience.

But together, we are all the more immortal now. This story is an extension of us. It only exists because I have made you perceive that it does. It is only the way that it is because of who you are.

Every time someone reads what we have created, we become more real. We thread ourselves into the consciousness of another person, creating a tapestry of ourselves, something familiar, within the infinite chaos. We become a greater part of reality, of meaning, of existence itself — fighting desperately against death and screaming together from the boundless silences of infinite time.

We were here! We were real!

Eventually, only the echoes of who we were will survive but they will still be ours. After all, who are any of us, other than an endless chain of outstretched pieces, like the universe itself.

END

There is very little that everyone can agree about when it comes to this bizarre, magical and transformative book.

But perhaps, if you have come this far, you can agree that it deserves to be shared.

So please, tell others. Leave a review. Create a tapestry of yourself within the infinite chaos.